WE'RE WITH YOU

WE'RE WITH YOU

Counsel and Encouragement from Your Brethren

DESERET
BOOK

SALT LAKE CITY, UTAH

Royalties from the sale of this book
will be donated to the General Missionary Fund of
The Church of Jesus Christ of Latter-day Saints

Compilation © 2016 Deseret Book Company

Library of Congress Cataloging-in-Publication Data

Names: The Church of Jesus Christ of Latter-day Saints. First Presidency, issuing body. | Council of the Twelve Apostles (The Church of Jesus Christ of Latter-day Saints), issuing body.
Title: We're with you : counsel and encouragement from your brethren.
Description: Salt Lake City, Utah : Deseret Book, [2016] | Includes bibliographical references.
Identifiers: LCCN 2016033761 | ISBN 9781629722894 (paperbound)
Subjects: LCSH: Christian life–Mormon authors. | The Church of Jesus Christ of Latter-day Saints–Doctrines. | Mormon Church–Doctrines. | LCGFT: Quotations.
Classification: LCC BX8656 .W47 2016 | DDC 248.4/89332–dc23
LC record available at https://lccn.loc.gov/2016033761

Printed in the United States of America
LSC Communications, Crawfordsville, IN

10   9   8   7   6   5   4   3

CONTENTS

WE'RE
WITH
YOU

This is your world.

The future is

in your hands.

The outcome is
up to you.

—President Thomas S. Monson

A SHINING LIGHT
President Thomas S. Monson

Each of you is one of a kind. Each has had experiences unique to you and you alone. We come from varied backgrounds. And yet there is much that we have in common one with another. We know where we came from, why we are here, and where we will go when we leave this life. We know that we are children of our Heavenly Father and that He loves us. We know we want to return to Him after we leave this earthly existence. We know that what we do—and don't do—here in mortality is of utmost importance. We also know that, should we fall short, our Savior has provided us with the precious gift of the Atonement and that, if we change our lives and our hearts and take advantage of the power of the Atonement, our sins and shortcomings will be forgiven and forgotten.

Our opportunities to shine are limitless. They surround us each day, in whatever circumstance we find ourselves. As we follow the example of the Savior, ours will be the opportunity to be a light, as it were, in the lives of those around us—whether they be our own family members, our coworkers, mere acquaintances, or total strangers.

I want you to know that I can feel your collective goodness.

You are choice sons and daughters of our Father in Heaven. Just think how much good can come to the world from our collective lights as we allow the gospel to radiate through us.

YOUR GENERATION
Elder Quentin L. Cook

As I have reflected on who you are, the feeling has come over me that you might not fully appreciate the significance of your generation. Society in general has given labels to various generations that are alive today. The oldest among us in the United States and other countries have been labeled the "Greatest Generation" because of what they endured in the worldwide Great Depression of the 1930s and then accomplished in World War II and its aftermath in building a better world. A number of the senior Brethren of the Church participated in these events.

Your generation, born in the 1980s and early- to mid-1990s, is currently referred to as the "Millennial Generation." Some commentators are skeptical about what your generation will accomplish. I believe you have the background and the foundation to be the best generation ever, particularly in advancing our Father in Heaven's plan.

Why do I say this? Your generation has had more exposure

to seminary and institute teaching than previous generations, and you have had the best training of any generation from Primary, priesthood, and Young Women. In addition, approximately 375,000 of you have served or are serving as missionaries. You represent over one-third of all of the missionaries who have served in this dispensation. For those of you who have not had the opportunity to serve a mission, your contribution, nevertheless, can be significant. Almost half of the First Presidency and the Twelve did not have the opportunity to serve a mission.

Please know that we have great confidence in you. The leadership of the Church honestly believes that you can build the kingdom like no previous generation. You have not only our love and confidence but also our prayers and blessings. We know that the success of your generation is essential to the continued establishment of the Church and the growth of the kingdom.

THE LORD KNOWS YOU
President Dieter F. Uchtdorf

It always lifts my spirits to be surrounded by the young adults of the Church, and you inspire me to declare, "Let Zion in her beauty rise" (*Hymns* [1985], no. 41). As you are living all around the world, you represent in a beautiful way the future and strength of the Church. Because of your righteous desires and your commitment to follow the Savior, the future of this Church looks bright.

My dear young friends, you are the hope of Israel. We love you. The Lord knows you; He loves you. The Lord has great confidence in you. He knows your successes, and He is mindful of your challenges and questions in life.

It is my prayer that you will seek the truth earnestly and unceasingly, that you will yearn to drink from the fount of all truth, whose waters are pure and sweet, "a well of water springing up into everlasting life" (John 4:14).

TRUE MILLENNIALS
President Russell M. Nelson

Many people refer to you as *Millennials.* I'll admit that when researchers refer to you by that word and describe what their studies reveal about you—your likes and dislikes, your feelings and inclinations, your strengths and weaknesses—I'm uncomfortable. There is something about the way they use the term *Millennial* that bothers me. And frankly, I am less interested in what the *experts* have to say about you than what the Lord has told me about you.

When I pray about you and ask the Lord how *He* feels about you, I feel something far different from what the researchers say.

Spiritual impressions I've received about you lead me to believe that the term *Millennial* may actually be perfect for you—but for a much different reason than the experts may ever understand.

The term *Millennial* is perfect for you if that term reminds you of who you *really* are and what your purpose in life *really* is. A True Millennial is one who was taught and did teach the gospel of Jesus Christ premortally and who made covenants with our Heavenly Father there about courageous things—even *morally* courageous things—that you would do while here on earth.

A True Millennial is a man or woman whom God trusted enough to send to earth during the most compelling dispensation in the history of this world. A True Millennial is a man or woman who lives now to help prepare the people of this world for the Second Coming of Jesus Christ and His millennial reign. Make no mistake about it—you were born to be a True Millennial.

YOUR CENTURY
Elder M. Russell Ballard

While it is not possible for me to shake hands with you and look you in the eye personally, I want you to know that you are precious in the sight of your Heavenly Father. He loves you. The leaders of the Church love you.

I look at you and see the future of the Church—not just

Do you know who you are?
Do you know what you have
been given and what a glorious
future you have? We are told
we are children of God. We
sing about it in Primary. We
say it to others, hoping they
will understand and believe it.
But do we really know what
it means?

—ELDER ROBERT D. HALES

the future bishops, stake presidents, mission presidents, and auxiliary leaders, but the great ranks of future mothers and fathers, Primary and Sunday School teachers, youth leaders, home teachers, visiting teachers, Scout leaders, choir directors, and countless others who will serve the Lord in the twenty-first century.

It will be a different century from the one before it. In some ways it will be better; in other ways it will be much more difficult for you and for your children. But one thing is inescapable: it will be *your* century—one in which you have the opportunity to leave your mark for good or otherwise. You will try to influence others, and others will try to influence you. Either you will share and promote your core values, rooted in the restored gospel of Jesus Christ, or you will allow others to define your values for you and your posterity.

CHILDREN OF THE COVENANT
Elder Neil L. Andersen

You and I are "children of the covenant" (3 Nephi 20:26). The Savior has declared it, and I confirm it to you. As we come to understand what it means, we see more clearly. Mortality comes more into focus.

It is not by chance that we find ourselves within this holy

lineage, the blood of Israel, with a promise and a destiny that through our lives and the lives of our posterity all the peoples of the earth will be blessed (see 1 Nephi 15:18; 3 Nephi 16:5-7; D&C 39:11).

When we see ourselves in the perspective of this holy family, those who came before us and those who come after us become very important to us. Now you might say, "But my parents and grandparents were not members of the Church." Or, "They were not faithful in the Church." Or, as a man in Argentina whom I called to be a stake president said to me: "I don't even know who my father is." He had been given the family name of his mother. He had not heard the name of the Church until he was eighteen years old. How could he be part of this royal family?

Through miraculous circumstances–which we will one day appreciate more than we can now explain–each of us has been brought into this covenant family, and we have become children of the covenant. It is not necessary that we be able to explain every detail. Here is where we reverse "seeing is believing" to "believing is the beginning of seeing." I confirm to you that it is not by chance that we are here and that we are who we are.

DON'T WEAR A MASK
Elder Quentin L. Cook

In view of the enormous potential for good that you possess, what are my concerns for your future? What counsel can I give you? First, there will be great pressure on you to act out of character—to even wear a mask—and become someone who doesn't really reflect who you are or who you want to be.

Once, in our capacities in public affairs, I went with some of the Brethren to meet with Abraham Foxman, the national director of the Anti-Defamation League. Its mission is to stop the defamation of the Jewish people. I asked him what counsel he would have for us in connection with our responsibilities in public affairs for the Church. He pondered for a moment and then explained the importance of encouraging people to not wear masks. He described the Ku Klux Klan. It was an organization that was very influential and quite frightening to most Americans in the first part of the last century. With identical robes and masks that made it impossible to identify the participants, they burned crosses on the lawns of those they targeted and appointed themselves as so-called moral watchdogs. Mr. Foxman pointed out that a minority of the Ku Klux Klan would have been the type to become brown-shirted bullies in the dictatorships of 1930s Europe, but the majority of them, without the masks, were usually normal people, including businessmen and churchgoers. He noted that hiding their identity and wearing a mask enabled them to participate in activities that they would normally have avoided. Their conduct had a terrible impact on American society.

Mr. Foxman's counsel was to stress the importance of people avoiding masks that hide their true identity.

Now, I am not suggesting that any of you would be involved in the kind of terrible events I have just described. I do believe, in our day, when being anonymous is easier than ever, that there are important principles involved in not wearing a mask and being "true to the faith . . . for which martyrs have perished" (*Hymns* [1985], no. 254).

One of your greatest protections against making bad choices is to not put on any mask of anonymity. If you ever find yourself wanting to do so, please know it is a serious sign of danger and one of the adversary's tools to get you to do something you should not do.

RECOGNIZING SPIRITUAL PROMPTINGS

The invitation to trust the Lord does not relieve us from the responsibility to know for ourselves. This is more than an opportunity; it is an obligation—and it is one of the reasons we were sent to this earth.

Latter-day Saints are accept everything

not asked to blindly
they hear.

We are encouraged to think and discover truth for ourselves. We are expected to ponder, to search, to evaluate, and thereby to come to a personal knowledge of the truth.

—President Dieter F. Uchtdorf

GETTING ANSWERS TO QUESTIONS
President Russell M. Nelson

Our Heavenly Father and His Son stand ready to respond to your questions through the ministering of the Holy Ghost. But it is up to you to learn how to qualify for and receive those answers.

Where can you start? Begin by spending more time in holy places. The temple is a holy place. So is the chapel, where you make new sacramental covenants each Sunday. I invite you also to make your apartment, your dorm, your home, or your room a holy place where you can safely retreat from the dark distractions of the world.

Prayer is a key. Pray to know what to stop doing and what to start doing. Pray to know what to add to your environment and what to remove so the Spirit can be with you in abundance.

Serve with love. Loving service to those who have lost their way or who are wounded in spirit opens your heart to personal revelation.

Spend more time—much more time—in places where the Spirit is present. That means more time with friends who are seeking to have the Spirit with them. Spend more time on your knees in prayer, more time in the scriptures, more time in family history work, more time in the temple. I promise you that as you consistently give the Lord a generous portion of your time, He will multiply the remainder.

BE STILL, AND KNOW
Elder M. Russell Ballard

People living in the past enjoyed an abundance of natural heavenly light and comfortable darkness, without streetlights, headlights, and light pollution found in all our cities across the world. In the cities of today, it is almost impossible to see the night sky as Abraham, Moses, Ruth, Elisabeth, Jesus, and the early Latter-day Saints did.

They also enjoyed a natural silence, with few man-made sounds interrupting their days and especially their nights. Modern noise from cars, planes, and something some of you may refer to as music has completely drowned out the natural world.

Finally, the people of earlier times experienced solitude in ways we cannot imagine in our crowded and busy world. Even when we are alone today, we can be tuned in with our handheld devices, laptops, and TVs to keep us entertained and occupied.

As an Apostle, I now ask you a question: Do you have any personal quiet time? I have wondered if those who lived in the past had more opportunity than we do now to see, feel, and experience the presence of the Spirit in their lives.

Seemingly, as our world gets brighter, louder, and busier, we have a greater challenge feeling the Spirit in our lives. If your life is void of quiet time, would you begin today to seek for some?

Everyone needs time to meditate and contemplate. Even the Savior of the world, during His mortal ministry, found time to do so: "And when he had sent the multitudes away, he went up into a mountain apart to pray: and when the evening was come, he was there alone" (Matthew 14:23).

We all need time to ask ourselves questions or to have a regular personal interview with ourselves. We are often so busy and the world is so loud that it is difficult to hear the heavenly words "be still, and know that I am God" (Psalm 46:10).

UNDERSTANDING
Elder Gary E. Stevenson

As a young missionary in Japan struggling to learn a difficult language, I heard some vocabulary words early and often. Greetings such as *ohayo gozaimasu* or *konnichiwa* were two of these. Another was *wakarimasen*, "I don't understand." This word, along with a side-to-side hand expression, seems to be a favorite response from Japanese contacts, directed to young missionaries as they attempt to strike up conversations.

Initially, as I reflected on the meaning of the scriptural passage that admonishes, "and with all thy getting get understanding" (Proverbs 4:7), I thought of *understanding* more in terms of this type of comprehension—what I might hear with my ears and understand in my mind. I thought of the Japanese saying, "*Wakarimasen*": Do I understand or not understand? "And with all thy getting get understanding"—or make certain to obtain a higher level of comprehension. However, as I have studied and observed the use of the word *understanding* in the scriptures or from the words of living prophets, I have come to realize a deeper meaning. Consider these words from Elder Robert D. Hales when he was the Presiding Bishop:

"First, we start with the intelligence with which we were born. To our intelligence we add knowledge as we search for answers, study, and educate ourselves. To our knowledge we add experience, which should lead us to a level of wisdom. In addition to our wisdom, we add the help of the Holy Ghost through our prayers of faith, asking for spiritual guidance and strength. Then, and only then, do we reach an understanding in our hearts—which motivates us to 'do what is right; let the consequence follow.' (*Hymns* [1985], no. 237.) The feelings of an understanding heart give us the sweet spirit of assurance of not only knowing but doing what is right no matter what the circumstances. The understanding in our hearts comes from a close interdependence of study and prayer" ("Making Righteous Choices at the Crossroads of Life," *Ensign,* November 1988, 10).

Now consider again: "And with all thy getting get understanding." Understanding in this context follows intelligence, knowledge, experience, wisdom, and promptings from the Holy Ghost—all of which lead us to understanding or to know and do what is right.

As we trust and rely on the Lord, a greater measure of understanding comes from Him into our heart.

THE SPIRIT OF REVELATION
Elder Jeffrey R. Holland

Revelation almost always comes in response to a question, usually an urgent question—not always, but usually. In that sense it does provide information, but it is urgently needed information, special information. For example, Moses's challenge at the Red Sea was how to get himself and the children of Israel out of the horrible predicament they were in. There were chariots behind them, sand dunes on every side, and just a lot

Jobs, assignments, contentions, and moves from here to there will lap at your feet to distract you and consume you. It is the way of mortality. Be wise. Know that you can draw upon the power of God to always have His Spirit with you on this journey.

—ELDER RONALD A. RASBAND

of water immediately ahead. He needed information all right—what to do—but it wasn't a casual thing he was asking. In this case it was literally a matter of life and death.

You will need information too, but in matters of great consequence it is not likely to come unless you want it urgently, faithfully, humbly. Moroni calls it seeking "with real intent" (Moroni 10:4). If you can seek that way, and stay in that mode, not much that the adversary can counter with will dissuade you from a righteous path. You can hang on, whatever the assault and affliction, because you have paid the price to—figuratively, at least—see the face of God and live.

There may come after the fact some competing doubts and some confusion, but they will pale when you measure them against the real thing. *Remember the real thing.* Remember how urgently you have needed help in earlier times and that you got it. The Red Sea will open to the honest seeker of revelation. The adversary does have power to hedge up the way, to marshal Pharaoh's forces and dog our escape right to the water's edge, but he can't produce the real thing. *He cannot conquer if we will it otherwise.*

THE POWER OF YOUR PRAYERS
President Dieter F. Uchtdorf

With the right attitude, you will be able to effectively communicate with your Heavenly Father, and not to just say your prayers. You will be able to say prayers that will go beyond the ceiling of the room–prayers not filled with trite repetitions or spoken without thinking but filled with your deep yearning to be one with your Father in Heaven.

In order to lift, enhance, and cultivate your relationship with God as His spiritual children, you have the unique opportunity to converse with the supreme source of wisdom and compassion in the universe.

Daily, simple but sincere and mighty prayers will help you to lift your lives onto a higher spiritual altitude. In your prayers you praise God, give thanks to Him, confess weaknesses, petition needs, and express deep devotion to your Heavenly Father. As you do this, in the name of Jesus Christ, the Redeemer, you perform a spiritual effort that leads to increased inspiration, revelation, and righteousness–not self-righteousness–and brings the brightness of heaven into your lives.

WHEN WE DON'T RECEIVE REVELATION
Elder Dallin H. Oaks

What about those times when we seek revelation and do not receive it? We do not always receive inspiration or revelation when we request it. Sometimes we are delayed in the receipt of revelation, and sometimes we are left to our own judgment. We cannot force spiritual things. It must be so. Our life's purpose to obtain experience and to develop faith would be frustrated if our Heavenly Father directed us in every act, even in every important act. We must make decisions and experience the consequences in order to develop self-reliance and faith.

Even in decisions we think very important, we sometimes receive no answers to our prayers. This does not mean that our prayers have not been heard. It only means that we have prayed about a decision which, for one reason or another, we should make without guidance by revelation.

No answer is likely to come to a person who seeks guidance in choosing between two alternatives that are equally acceptable to the Lord. Thus, there are times when we can serve productively in two different fields of labor. Either answer is right. When a choice will make a real difference in our lives–obvious or not—and when we are living in tune with the Spirit and seeking His guidance, we can be sure we will receive the guidance we need to attain our goal.

RECOGNIZING WHEN THE HOLY GHOST IS SPEAKING
Elder David A. Bednar

Because the Holy Ghost typically uses our minds and our hearts to convey spiritual messages, it can sometimes be difficult to discern the difference between our own thoughts and feelings and those communicated from our Heavenly Father. May I suggest four principles that can help us to receive, recognize, and respond to the Holy Ghost in our daily lives.

Principle #1: We must desire the companionship of the Holy Ghost.

Simply stated, we must desire, yearn for, and seek the companionship of the Holy Ghost. Do you and I remember to pray, both morning and night, for that which we should most desire, even the Holy Ghost? Or do we get caught up in the routine of daily living and the cares of the world and neglect this most valuable of all gifts? Receiving, recognizing, and responding to the Holy Ghost starts with our sincere and constant desire for His companionship and influence in our lives.

Principle #2: We must invite the companionship of the Holy Ghost.

We receive more readily and recognize more clearly the influence of the Holy Ghost as we specifically invite Him into our lives. We cannot compel or coerce or command the Holy Ghost. We must invite Him into our lives with the same gentleness and tenderness by which He influences us. Frankly, I am troubled by frequently repeated language that suggests we can "call down the powers of heaven." Certainly we can invite such power, but I would never suggest we can "call it down" according to our will and timing.

Our invitations for the companionship of the Holy Ghost can occur in many ways. We invite the Holy Ghost into our lives through the making and keeping of sacred covenants. Meaningful personal prayer every morning and every night invites the Holy Ghost into our lives. Searching the scriptures daily and diligently invites the Holy Ghost into our lives. Sincere worship in our homes and at Church invites the Holy Ghost into our lives.

Principle #3: We must heed simple promptings.

We are prompted by the Holy Ghost every day to do ordinary and simple things. For example, we are prompted to say our personal prayers every morning and every night. We are prompted to study the scriptures. To the degree that we heed these simple promptings, then our capacity to recognize and respond to the Holy Ghost is increased. To the degree that we do not heed these simple promptings, then our capacity to recognize and respond to the Holy Ghost is decreased. We are either progressing or regressing in our ability to recognize and respond to the Holy Ghost. There is no neutral ground; there is no standing still.

Principle #4: We must heed promptings quickly.

Have you ever received and recognized a prompting from the Holy Ghost, and then decided to respond to it *later*? And then when later arrived, you found that you could not remember the prompting. I have learned that acting upon promptings quickly greatly increases our capacity to receive and recognize the influence of the Holy Ghost. I have also learned that properly recording spiritual impressions demonstrates to the Savior how much I treasure His direction. The simple practice of writing down spiritual thoughts and feelings greatly enhances the likelihood of receiving and recognizing additional promptings from the Holy Ghost.

ENGAGING WITH GOD'S WORD

CHAPTER 2

A farmer cannot expect to harvest in the fall
if he does not properly sow in the spring and
work hard during the summer to weed, nourish,
and cultivate the field. So it is for you and me.

We cannot expect
insight unless we
of regular and

to reap scriptural pay the price diligent study.

Casual strolling through or dabbling in the scriptures will not yield enduring gospel understanding.

—Elder David A. Bednar

READING, STUDYING, AND SEARCHING
Elder David A. Bednar

I want to review with you three basic ways or methods of obtaining living water from the scriptural reservoir: (1) *reading* the scriptures from beginning to end, (2) *studying* the scriptures by topic, and (3) *searching* the scriptures for connections, patterns, and themes. Each of these approaches can help satisfy our spiritual thirst if we invite the companionship and assistance of the Holy Ghost as we read, study, and search.

Reading a book of scripture from beginning to end initiates the flow of living water into our lives by introducing us to important stories, gospel doctrines, and timeless principles. This approach also enables us to learn about major characters in the scriptures and the sequence, timing, and context of events and teachings. Reading the written word in this way exposes us to the breadth of a volume of scripture. This is the first and most fundamental way of obtaining living water.

Studying by topic typically follows, grows out of, and builds upon our reading of the scriptures from beginning to end. For example, as we read the Book of Mormon we may identify and seek to find answers to important doctrinal and practical questions such as these:

- What is faith in the Savior?
- Why is faith in Jesus Christ the first principle of the gospel?
- Why and how does faith in the Redeemer lead to repentance?
- How does the Atonement strengthen me to do things in my daily life that I could never do with my own limited capacity and in my own strength?

Focusing upon such questions and studying by topic, using the Topical Guide and index to the triple combination, allow us to dig into and explore the depth of the scriptures and obtain a much richer spiritual knowledge. This approach increases the rate at which living water flows into our lives.

Both reading from beginning to end and studying by topic are prerequisites to the third basic method of obtaining living water from the scriptural reservoir. Whereas reading a book of scripture from beginning to end provides a basic breadth of knowledge, studying by topic increases the depth of our knowledge. *Searching* in the revelations for connections, patterns, and themes builds upon and adds to our spiritual knowledge by bringing together and expanding these first two methods; it broadens our perspective and understanding of the plan of salvation.

In my judgment, diligently searching to discover connections, patterns, and themes is in part what it means to "feast" upon the words of Christ. This approach can open the floodgates of the spiritual reservoir, enlighten our understanding through His Spirit, and produce a depth of gratitude for the holy scriptures and a degree of spiritual commitment that can be received in no other way. Such searching enables us to build upon the rock of our Redeemer and to withstand the winds of wickedness in these latter days.

BUILDING FAITH WITH THE SCRIPTURES
President Thomas S. Monson

It is up to each of us to develop the faith necessary to survive spiritually and to project a light for others to see. Amidst the confusion of our age, the conflicts of conscience, and the turmoil of daily living, an abiding faith becomes an anchor to our lives. Remember that faith and doubt cannot exist in the same mind at the same time, for one will dispel the other. Among the most effective ways to gain and keep the faith we need would be to read and study the scriptures and to pray frequently and consistently.

Many years ago I was shown the flyleaf of a triple

combination given to the late Maurine Lee Wilkins by her father, President Harold B. Lee. He had inscribed it with these words:

"April 9, 1944–To my dear Maurine: That you may have a constant measure by which to judge between truth and the errors of man's philosophies, and thus grow in spirituality as you increase in knowledge, I give you this sacred book to read frequently and cherish throughout your life. Lovingly, your father, Harold B. Lee"

Wise words which can apply to each of us.

Brothers and sisters, many of you probably already know that the Book of Mormon is true, that Joseph Smith is indeed a prophet, and that this is the true Church of Jesus Christ. Some of you, however, may still be living on the testimony of others–your parents, your friends, your Church leaders. May I suggest that you set aside time every day to find out for yourself if the Book of Mormon is a true book, for it will change your heart and change your life. If you seek this knowledge "with a sincere heart, with real intent, having faith in Christ" (Moroni 10:4), I promise that you will receive an answer. And once you know that the Book of Mormon is true, then it will follow that Joseph Smith was a prophet of God. You will have that burning testimony and knowledge that this Church is true. Such knowledge, such a personal testimony, is essential if we are to safely navigate the sometimes treacherous paths through life with the adversary attempting to deceive us at every turn.

HUNGERING FOR THE WORD
Elder Jeffrey R. Holland

King Benjamin's sermon—for which he had to bring people together in such a crowd that they could not all see him or hear him, for which he had to build a tower and distribute a multilithed text of his talk—gave us the first example of the Conference Report, I suppose. That's part of the reason we have the *Ensign*. Every May and November we have a new religious text. Like King Benjamin, our prophet wants the text to be heard and to be read. If we're not all able to crowd into the Conference Center, as King Benjamin's people were not, then it is important that we see and hear and read as much as we can. The Conference Report becomes scripture to us in our own day. Christ, on both continents, held those kinds of conferences—on mountaintops, by the seashore, in a boat, in an upper room. He held them almost anywhere and everywhere because the people hungered and thirsted for the kind of message that comes by the voice of the Lord.

I remember a trip I made to Vavau, Tonga, in the 1970s. It is a little island that is one and a half hours away from Nuku'alofa by plane and twenty-four hours away by boat. By boat it is the worst trip that can be made. When the area conference was announced for Tonga, it was determined that only one boat would be available for the Saints from Vavau. The boat held 150 people. If you stuffed bodies into every possible corner of the ship, you could get close to three hundred people. *Eight hundred Tongans jammed onto that boat* and stood up for twenty-four hours without sleep, without food, without drink, without anything–because they knew that a prophet of God was going to be in their islands and they were not going to miss him for anything in the world.

A SENSE OF THE SACRED
Elder D. Todd Christofferson

We hold in our hands a considerable volume of scripture. The records stretch back to the early patriarchs and forward to our own lifetimes. I suppose this is more scripture than has ever been had by a people in history, and certainly it is more widely available than ever scripture was in the past. I am sure that if you or I held in our hands the original scrolls that Moses wrote upon or the very metal plates that Mormon had inscribed, we would feel a deep sense of reverence and awe and would treat those objects with great care. And so we should, because they are sacred objects, made so in part by the labor and sacrifice of the holy prophets who so painstakingly prepared them.

But the greatest value of such scrolls or plates is not in the objects themselves but in the words they contain. They are sacred because they are the words of God, and while we may not hold the original documents, we do hold the words. Therefore, what we have is holy—holy writ.

Having been granted possession of the recorded words of God, we should ask ourselves if we are respecting the sacred nature of this record. Some have violated the sacredness of the scriptures by ridiculing or denying their validity. That, of course, is a very serious matter.

But for most of us, who readily acknowledge the truthfulness of the standard works, if we are ever guilty of disrespecting the sacred nature of scriptures, it is by neglect. The risk we must guard against day to day is the tendency to treat lightly, or even ignore, the sacred word.

A sense of the sacred includes an appreciation—even a love—of the scriptures. A sense of the sacred leads one to feast upon the words of Christ (see 2 Nephi 31:20; 32:3), which in turn deepens one's reverence for His words.

When we come to hear a servant of the Lord, we are not "to trifle with the words" that he speaks. It is our duty to open our ears to hear and our hearts to understand. And what we should seek to understand is what we should do about the message.

—ELDER DALLIN H. OAKS

RETURN TO THE SCRIPTURES
President Henry B. Eyring

I plead with you to do the simple things with determination that will move you forward spiritually.

Start with remembering Him. You will remember what you know and what you love. The Savior gave us the scriptures, paid for by prophets at a price we cannot measure, so that we could know Him. Lose yourself in them. Decide now to read more and more effectively than you have ever done before.

Just last month I learned again the power that comes from trying harder to have the scriptures opened to our hearts. It began when I noticed the scriptures of a man sitting next to me in a meeting. He opened them as the discussion progressed, and I could see that they were marked, as I had done, but with a difference. He had placed colored tags on the edges of pages, keyed to the colors in which he had marked the scriptures. I asked him after the meeting to tell me about it. He showed me the front of his scriptures where he had placed a typed page. On that page were topics about the gospel, each with a line under it. And he had placed the colored markers on the edge of the scriptures, one color for each topic, so that he could study all the scriptures that were helpful to him on that topic.

Within a day I had purchased an inexpensive set of scriptures. But it took more than a few days and more than a few prayers for me to know the topics that would open the scriptures anew for me. I chose the topics that would teach me of my call to be a witness of Jesus Christ. The first topic is the witness that Jesus Christ is the Son of God; the next is that He is risen; and the third is that He is the head of His Church. I would not urge you to buy a new set of scriptures, nor to get colored tags and colored pencils, nor to choose the topics that I chose. But I plead with you to return to the scriptures in some way that opens your mind and heart to be taught.

THE IRON ROD
Elder Neil L. Andersen

Nephi promised us that "whoso would hearken unto the word of God, and would hold fast unto it, . . . would never perish; neither could the temptations . . . of the adversary overpower them . . . , to lead them away to destruction" (1 Nephi 15:24).

The iron rod *is* the word of God. I like to think of it in this way: The word of God contains three very strong elements that intertwine and sustain one another to form an immovable rod. These three elements include, first, the scriptures, or the words of the ancient prophets. The second element of the word of God is the personal revelation and inspiration that comes to us through the Holy Ghost. The third part of the iron rod represents the words of the living prophets. We must also hold fast to the word of God as delivered by the living prophets. My prayer is that we will increase our attentiveness to what the living prophets are teaching, accelerate our response to what we are learning, and deepen our understanding of what it means to *hold fast* to their words.

Whenever the Lord's Church has been established, the Lord has called prophets and apostles. The Savior said, "Ye have not chosen me, but I have chosen you, and ordained you" (John 15:16). To these men that ordination brings a spiritual power and a solemn responsibility–a power to know and to testify and a responsibility to teach and to bless. It also brings a responsibility and a promise to us. We have the responsibility to listen and to follow, and we have a promise that blessings will come as we believe and act on their words.

When the Lord called twelve disciples in the Americas after His Resurrection, He taught the people this: "Blessed are ye if ye shall give heed unto the words of these twelve whom I have chosen from among you to minister unto you, and to be your servants" (3 Nephi 12:1). In our day, in a very difficult time, the Lord promised the Saints: "If my people will hearken unto my voice, and unto the voice of my servants whom I have appointed to lead my people, behold, verily I say unto you, they shall not be moved out of their place" (D&C 124:45).

This is the Lord's pattern. He calls fifteen men and endows them with the keys and power to guide and direct us. We are not forced to obey; there is no compulsion. But if we will be attentive to their words, if we will be responsive and willing to change our behavior as the Holy Ghost confirms their counsel, we will not be moved out of our place—meaning we will hold fast to the iron rod and will forever remain safely on the path leading to the tree of life.

Our own faith in the Savior grows and develops through the times and seasons of our lives. There may be moments of doubt or discouragement when we feel as though we are enveloped in the mists of darkness. Do not underestimate what we each can receive from the solemn, sure testimony of the Savior borne by His special witnesses. That witness, received in a spirit of faith, will strengthen us in moments of difficulty and give us a firm footing as we move along the path toward the tree of life. Hold fast to the words of the prophets. Ponder them. Believe them. Trust them. Follow them.

IDENTIFYING

AND

DEFENDING

TRUTH

The beauty of the gospel of Jesus Christ is that it pours knowledge into our souls and shows things in their true light.

With that enhanced we can discern the choices before us

perspective,
more clearly
and their consequences.

We can, therefore, make more
intelligent use of our agency.

—Elder D. Todd Christofferson

ABSOLUTE TRUTH
Elder Dallin H. Oaks

We know that the existence of God and the existence of absolute truth are fundamental to life on this earth, whether they are believed or not. We also know that evil exists and that some things are simply, seriously, and everlastingly wrong. As an Apostle of the Lord Jesus Christ, I seek to help you make right choices in a world that is increasingly polarized between belief and disbelief, between good and evil.

It is well to worry about our moral foundation. We live in a world where more and more persons of influence are teaching and acting out a belief that there is no absolute right and wrong, that all authority and all rules of behavior are man-made choices that can prevail over the commandments of God. Many even question whether there is a God.

The philosophy of moral relativism, which holds that each person is free to choose for himself what is right and wrong, is becoming the unofficial creed for many in America and other Western nations. At the extreme level, evil acts that used to be localized and covered up like a boil are now legalized and paraded like a banner. Persuaded by this philosophy, many of the rising generation–youth and young adults–are caught up in self-serving pleasures, pagan painting and piercing of body parts, foul language, revealing attire, pornography, dishonesty, and degrading sexual indulgence.

Bible and Book of Mormon prophets foresaw this time, when men would be "lovers of pleasures more than lovers of God" (2 Timothy 3:4) and, indeed, when men would deny God (see Jude 1:4; 2 Nephi 28:5; Moroni 7:17; D&C 29:22).

In this troubled circumstance, we who believe in God and the corollary truth of absolute right and wrong have the challenge of living in a godless and increasingly amoral world. In this circumstance, all of us—and especially you of the rising generation—have a duty to stand up and speak up to affirm that God exists and that there are absolute truths His commandments establish.

DIVINE LAW
Elder D. Todd Christofferson

Not knowing the truth could lead us into serious error. There is a philosophy abroad in the world that, in essence, places man in the role of supreme being. This philosophy argues that there is no higher law than one's own preferences or feelings, one's own desires and opinions. Each person becomes a law unto himself or herself and should not be subject to any other authority. By this reasoning, whatever one feels is right for him is necessarily right, and the rest of the universe must acknowledge and accept that judgment. In Korihor's phrase, "whatsoever a man [does is] no crime" (Alma 30:17). No one can judge the right or wrong of another's choices.

People are not yet willing to accept the end result of this sophistry that would, for example, preclude punishment of a man who commits murder if he felt it was right for him to do it. We still want to define some actions as crimes and prohibit them because of their effects on others. But society has already moved a significant distance down the road toward nonjudgmental acceptance of any and all behavior. Adultery is no longer considered a crime in many jurisdictions despite its devastating impact on others, especially innocent parties. It is preached that such conduct is a personal choice, and the participants decide whether it is right or wrong for them. I have read of students who in their own minds cannot condemn the Nazi Holocaust because to do so would be imposing their values on others—something strictly forbidden by this code of moral relativism. Presumably such persons would not oppose any future genocide. The philosophy that makes each man or woman his or her own lawgiver clearly leads to a lawless and dismal end.

TRUTH AND HUMAN WISDOM
President Dieter F. Uchtdorf

Part of our problem in the quest for truth is that human wisdom has disappointed us so often. We have so many examples of things that mankind once "knew" were true but have since been proven false. For example, in spite of one-time overwhelming consensus, the earth isn't flat. The stars don't revolve around the earth. Eating a tomato will not cause instant death. And, of course, man actually can fly—even break the sound barrier.

The "truths" we cling to shape the quality of our societies as well as our individual characters. All too often these "truths" are based on incomplete and inaccurate evidence, and at times they serve very selfish motives.

Part of the reason for poor judgment comes from the tendency of mankind to blur the line between belief and truth. We too often confuse belief with truth, thinking that because something makes sense or is convenient, it must be true. Conversely, we sometimes don't believe truth or reject it—because it would require us to change or admit that we were wrong. Often, truth is rejected because it doesn't appear to be consistent with previous experiences.

When the opinions or "truths" of others contradict our own, instead of considering the possibility that there could be information that might be helpful and augment or complement what we know, we often jump to conclusions or make assumptions that the other person is misinformed, mentally challenged, or even intentionally trying to deceive. Unfortunately, this tendency can spread to all areas of our lives—from sports to family relationships and from religion to politics.

My young friends, as you accept the responsibility to seek after truth with an open mind and a humble heart, you will become more tolerant of others, more open to listen, more prepared to understand, more inclined to build up instead of tearing down, and more willing to go where the Lord wants you to go.

DEFENDING TRUTH IN THE PUBLIC SQUARE
Elder Dallin H. Oaks

When believers in Jesus Christ take their views of truth into the public square, they must seek the inspiration of the Lord to be selective and wise in choosing which true principles they seek to promote by law or executive action. Generally, they should refrain from seeking laws or administrative action to facilitate beliefs that are distinctive to believers, such as the

How do you respond to moments of truth in your life? There is a considerable difference between sitting and doing nothing, and standing and doing what is right.

—ELDER GARY E. STEVENSON

enforcement of acts of worship, even by implication. Believers can be less cautious in seeking government action that would serve principles broader than merely facilitating the practice of their beliefs, such as laws concerning public health, safety, and morals.

When believers seek to promote their positions in the public square, their methods and their advocacy should always be tolerant of the opinions and positions of others who do not share their beliefs. We should not add to the extremism that divides our society. As believers, we must always speak with love and show patience, understanding, and compassion toward our adversaries. Christian believers are under command to love their neighbors (see Luke 10:27), to forgive (see Matthew 18:21-35), and to do good to those who despitefully use them (see Matthew 5:44).

As believers, we should also frame our arguments and positions in ways that contribute to the reasoned discussion and accommodation that are essential to democratic government in a pluralistic society. By this means we will contribute to the civility that is essential to preserve our civilization.

Believers should not be deterred by the familiar charge that they are trying to legislate morality. Many areas of the law are based on Judeo-Christian morality and have been for centuries. Our civilization is based on morality and cannot exist without it.

We Latter-day Saints are sometimes accused of being self-righteous and intolerant of others, especially where we are in the majority or where others are in the majority and our beliefs cause us to oppose them. Surely Latter-day Saints do need to be more wise and skillful in explaining and pursuing our views and in exercising our influence when we have it.

HOW CAN WE FIND TRUTH?
President Dieter F. Uchtdorf

The thing about truth is that it exists beyond belief. It is true even if nobody believes it.

We can say west is north and north is west all day long and even believe it with all our heart, but if, for example, we want to fly from Quito, Ecuador, to New York City in the United States, there is only one direction that will lead us there, and that is north. West just won't do.

Of course, this is just a simple aviation analogy. However, there is indeed such a thing as absolute truth—unassailable, unchangeable truth. This truth is different from belief. It is different from hope. Absolute truth is not dependent upon public opinion or popularity. Polls cannot sway it. Not even the inexhaustible authority of celebrity endorsement can change it.

So how can we find truth?

I believe that our Father in Heaven is pleased with His children when they use their talents and mental faculties to earnestly discover truth. Over the centuries many wise men and women–through logic, reason, scientific inquiry, and, yes, through inspiration–have discovered truth. These discoveries have enriched mankind, improved our lives, and inspired joy, wonder, and awe. Even so, the things we once thought we knew are continually being enhanced, modified, or even contradicted by enterprising scholars who seek to understand truth.

The adversary has many cunning strategies for keeping mortals from the truth. He offers the belief that truth is relative; appealing to our sense of tolerance and fairness, he keeps the real truth hidden by claiming that one person's "truth" is as valid as any other.

Some he entices to believe that there is an absolute truth out there somewhere but that it is impossible for anyone to know it.

For those who already embrace the truth, his primary strategy is to spread the seeds of doubt. For example, he has caused many members of the Church to stumble when they discover information about the Church that seems to contradict what they had learned previously. If you experience such a moment, remember that in this age of information there are many who create doubt about anything and everything, at any time and every place. And it is always good to keep in mind that just because something is printed on paper, appears on the Internet, is frequently repeated, or has a powerful group of followers doesn't make it true.

Our world is full of confusion. But eventually all of our questions will be answered. All of our doubts will be replaced by certainty. And that is because there is one source of truth that is complete, correct, and incorruptible. That source is our infinitely wise and all-knowing Heavenly Father. He knows truth as it was, as it is, and as it yet will be (see D&C 93:24).

THE POWER OF THE TEMPLE

CHAPTER 4

The temple is a place of personal revelation.

If you are visit the temple

endowed,
regularly.

If you are not, prepare yourself to enter,
for inside the doors of the temple rests
the power that will fortify you against
the vicissitudes of life.

—Elder M. Russell Ballard

THE SAVING ORDINANCES OF THE TEMPLE
Elder Robert D. Hales

We have been taught in the scriptures that the personal worthiness required of us by the Lord to enter the temple and to take upon us the sacred covenants therein is one of the greatest blessings available to us in mortality. Then, after taking upon us the covenants in the temple, our obedience in living the covenants daily is a demonstration of our faith, love, devotion, and spiritual commitment to honor our Heavenly Father and His Son Jesus Christ and prepares us to live with Them in the eternities. The temple's saving ordinances are essential to—and even the central focus of—the eternal plan of happiness.

We need to acquire a testimony and a reverent feeling of the temple being the house of the Lord. The temple is truly a place where you are "in the world and not of the world." When you are troubled, and when you have crucial decisions that weigh heavily on your mind and soul, you can take your cares to the temple and receive spiritual guidance.

The temple is a sacred edifice, a holy place where essential saving ceremonies and ordinances are performed to prepare us for exaltation. It is important that we gain a sure knowledge that our preparation to enter the holy house and our participation in these ceremonies and covenants are some of the most significant events we will experience in our mortal lives.

Temples are the greatest university of learning known to man, giving us knowledge and wisdom about the creation of the world. Washings and anointings tell us who we are. Endowment instructions give guidance as to how we should conduct our lives here in mortality. We are taught in the scriptures that temples are "a place of instruction for all those who are called to the work of the ministry . . . ; That they may be perfected in [their] understanding . . . in all things pertaining to the kingdom of God on the earth" (D&C 97:13-14).

The primary purpose of the temple is to provide the ordinances necessary for our exaltation in the celestial kingdom. Temple ordinances guide us to our Savior and give us the blessings that come to us through the Atonement of Jesus Christ. The meaning of the word *endowment* is "gift." The ordinance consists of a series of instructions on how we should live and covenants we make to live righteously by following our Savior.

Another important ordinance is being sealed for eternity in celestial marriage. This covenant allows children to be sealed to their parents and children born in the covenant to become part of an eternal family. When a couple is kneeling at the altar, as a sealer I am aware of my role as a representative of the Lord. I know that what is sealed on earth is literally sealed in heaven—never to be broken if those being sealed remain faithful and endure to the end.

TEMPLES ANCIENT AND MODERN
President Russell M. Nelson

Temples are not new. "Whenever the Lord has had a people on the earth who will obey His word, they have been commanded to build temples" (Bible Dictionary, "Temple," 781). The Old Testament is replete with references to ordinances, covenants, and even the clothing of the temple (see, for example, Exodus 28-29; Leviticus 8).

As we read of temples, we also learn of covenants that God has made with faithful followers—His "children of the covenant" (3 Nephi 20:26). Some four thousand years ago, God made a covenant with Abraham that all the nations of the earth will be blessed through his seed (see Genesis 17:7; 22:18; Abraham 2:9-11). It was reaffirmed with Isaac (see Genesis 26:1-4, 24) and again with Jacob (see Genesis 28; 35:9-13; 48:3-4). The thread of that covenant is woven throughout the entire fabric of the Old Testament, the New Testament, and the Book of Mormon (see, for example, Book of Mormon title page). That covenant has been divinely renewed in this dispensation as part of the Restoration of all things (see D&C 124:58).

Prophets have long known that the Abrahamic covenant was to be fulfilled *only* "in the latter days" (1 Nephi 15:18). That's our day! (See D&C 110:12-16.) We are those covenant people! In our holy temples, we literally receive those blessings promised to the lineage of Abraham, Isaac, and Jacob.

In the Restoration, temple work received a very high priority. The first revelation from a ministering angel pertained to this doctrine. Recorded in the second section of the Doctrine and Covenants, it is an echo of the fourth chapter of Malachi. Moroni foretold the coming of Elijah, who would turn the hearts of the fathers to the children and the hearts of the children to their fathers (see Malachi 4:5-6; D&C 2:1-2).

Elijah did come, on April 3, 1836. He came to the Kirtland Temple to confer keys of sealing authority, precisely as prophesied by the angel Moroni (see D&C 110:14-16).

In the temple, ordinances are administered through which the power of God is manifest (see D&C 84:20). Without those ordinances and the authority of the priesthood, "the power of godliness is not manifest unto men in the flesh" (D&C 84:21).

The inscription on modern temples reads, "Holiness to the Lord" (see Exodus 28:36; 39:30). Those words describe the building, yes. They also describe the ordinances and covenants of the temple and the people who worship within its walls.

FOCUS ON THE TEMPLE
Elder Quentin L. Cook

When my wife and I were starting out as a newly married couple in the San Francisco Bay Area in the mid-1960s, the LDS population was relatively small. In addition, that area had become a magnet for drug usage and all manner of promiscuous and sinful conduct. A concerned stake president back then asked the leadership of the Church if leaders should encourage Church members to remain in the San Francisco Bay Area. Elder Harold B. Lee, then a senior member of the Quorum of the Twelve, was assigned to address the issue. He met with a group of priesthood leaders and told them that the Lord had not inspired the construction of a temple in our area only to have the members leave. His counsel was:

1. To create Zion in our hearts and homes.

2. To be a light to those among whom we live.

3. To focus on the ordinances and principles taught in the temple.

In these times of commotion the Lord expects us to adjust our habits and be in His house more often.

If you will follow President Lee's counsel, you can success-fully be in the world but not of the world. However, we must each determine whether we will face the world or focus on the temple.

THE TEMPLE GROUNDS
Elder M. Russell Ballard

To help us discover the world where Adam and Eve, Abraham and Sarah, and Joseph and Mary found God, and to help us find a place to feel and hear the voice of the Lord today, I invite you to go to the temple. Go as often as you can, and turn off your smartphones and put them away before you enter the temple grounds.

In all the ordinances in the house of the Lord, you will hear beautiful language, words, and promises given by the Lord to His children. It is the only place you can hear those beautiful, inspiring words.

If you do not qualify for a temple recommend right now, visit the temple grounds. Let me make a very important point in case you have never heard it before: Nothing prevents you or anyone else from visiting the temple grounds. The Lord wants you to prepare yourself to be worthy of a temple recom-mend and come to the temple as soon as you can. Walking the grounds will plant in your heart a desire to get a recommend and attend the temple regularly.

Satan, on the other hand, does not want you to go to the temple or even to stand in the shadow of a temple. He wants you to avoid even getting close to the temple because the temple is the house of the Lord.

I assure each of you that as you go to the temple or visit the temple grounds, you will walk on sacred, holy ground just as the early patriarchs and matriarchs did so long ago. They were focused on their eternal journey and the most important things of life. Like them, you can also focus on feeling power and the presence of heaven.

If you choose, you can hear the still, small voice of the Spirit in the temple or on its sacred grounds in ways you never will at the mall, in restaurants, and in public places. In fact, you will find that the temple is a wonderful place to receive answers to your prayers.

LINKING THE GENERATIONS
Elder Neil L. Andersen

If we can look back through the generations, we see those who helped us to get where we are now—those who forged the way before us, whether they were members of the Church or

RIGHT MARGIN:

not. And in the restored gospel we realize even more deeply our responsibility to link them to us through the ordinances of the temple.

When we look at our own lives, we must be prepared to look forward into the generations that will follow us, for our footprints will be seen in homes and on paths where we will never walk. As we are righteous, there is a power in the priesthood that passes through us into our posterity, shaping their eternity as it shapes ours.

As you can learn to see through the generations–by looking back and by looking forward–you will see more clearly who you are and what you must become. You will better see that your place in this vast, beautiful plan of happiness is no small place. And you will come to love the Savior and depend on Him–as His great gift to us makes this all possible. Your influence will continue generation after generation throughout all eternity.

PREPARING FOR TEMPLE BLESSINGS
President Russell M. Nelson

To each young adult I emphasize that the temple can bless you–even before you enter it. By maintaining a standard of moral conduct high enough to qualify for a temple recommend, you will find inner peace and spiritual strength. Now is the time to cleanse your lives of anything that is displeasing to the Lord. Now is the time to eliminate feelings of envy or enmity and seek forgiveness for any offense.

Before you enter the temple for the first time, participation in a temple preparation seminar will help you understand the magnificence of the ordinances and covenants of the temple.

Plan now to be married in the temple, and conduct your courtship with the temple in mind. When you and your companion kneel at the altar of a holy temple, you do so as equal partners. You become an eternal family unit. Anything that might erode the spirituality, love, and sense of true partnership is contrary to the will of the Lord. Fidelity to these sacred ordinances and covenants will bring eternal blessings to you and to generations yet unborn.

UNCOVERING YOUR LIFE'S WORK

CHAPTER 5

This is your time.
What will you do with it?

Are you where
to be with

*you want
your life?*

If not, what are you
going to do about it?

—President Thomas S. Monson

CHANGES IN MY PLANS
Elder Dallin H. Oaks

When I was a young man I thought I would serve a mission. I graduated from high school in June 1950. Thousands of miles away, one week after that high school graduation, a North Korean army crossed the 38th parallel, and our country was at war. I was seventeen years old, but as a member of the Utah National Guard I was soon under orders to prepare for mobilization and active service. Suddenly, for me and for many other young men of my generation, the full-time mission we had planned or assumed was not to be.

Another example of a shift in my plans for my life: After I served as president of BYU for nine years, I was released. A few months later the governor of the state of Utah appointed me to a ten-year term on the supreme court of this state. I was then forty-eight years old. My wife June and I tried to plan the rest of our lives. We wanted to serve the full-time mission neither of us had been privileged to serve. We planned that I would serve twenty years on the state supreme court. Then, at the end of two ten-year terms, when I would be nearly sixty-nine years old, I would retire from the supreme court and we would submit our missionary papers and serve a mission as a couple.

Four years after we made that plan I was called to the Quorum of the Twelve Apostles—something we never dreamed would happen. Realizing then that the Lord had different plans and different timing than we had assumed, I resigned as a justice of the supreme court. But this was not the end of the important differences. When I was sixty-six, my wife June died of cancer. Two years later, I married Kristen McMain, the eternal companion who now stands at my side.

How fundamentally different my life is than I had sought to plan! My professional life has changed. My personal life has changed. But the commitment I made to the Lord—to put Him first in my life and to be ready for whatever He would have me do—has carried me through these changes of eternal importance.

BALANCING "GETTING" WITH "UNDERSTANDING"
Elder Gary E. Stevenson

Most of you are approaching or have entered a critical intersection or crossroads in your life. You are becoming more independent with each year of your life that passes, and you are moving deeper into the "and with all thy getting" phase of your life. What is it that you are going to be getting? It may be getting a husband or a wife, your own family, a car, a job, a salary, a house, and a mortgage, to name a few. In order to manage these very important things that we "get," one must also obtain "understanding," as the scripture teaches (Proverbs 4:7). This understanding comes through *an interdependence of study and prayer.* Said another way, one must have trust or reliance upon the Lord.

I have personally observed the heartbreak and personal havoc wrought upon those whose focus is on the worldly "getting" and not on the Lord's "understanding." It seems that those who lean unto their own understanding or rely on the arm of the flesh are more likely to develop a disproportionate focus on or obsession for material gain, prestige, power, and position. Keeping the "getting" in accordance with the scriptural guidance of "understanding" will temper your temporal appetite. This will allow the proper context for your activities as a productive member of society and of the Lord's kingdom.

THE IMPORTANCE OF GOALS
President Thomas S. Monson

It is necessary to prepare and to plan so that we don't fritter away our lives. Without a goal, there can be no real success. The best definition of success I have ever found goes something like this: "Success is the progressive realization of a worthy ideal." Someone has said that the trouble with not having a goal is that you can spend your life running up and down the field and never crossing the goal line.

Years ago there was a romantic and fanciful ballad titled "Wishing Will Make It So." I want to state here and now that wishing will not replace thorough preparation to meet the trials of life. Preparation is hard work, but it is absolutely essential for our progress.

Concerning your preparation, let me share with you this time-honored advice, which has never been more applicable than it is right now: It is not the number of hours you put in but what you put in the hours that counts.

Have discipline in your preparations. Have checkpoints where you can determine if you're on course. Study something you like and which will make it possible for you to support a family. While this counsel would apply almost certainly to every young man, it also has relevance to young women. There are situations in life that we cannot predict, situations that will require employable skills. You can't get the jobs of tomorrow until you have the skills of today. Business in the new economy, where the only guarantee is change, brings us to serious preparation.

Make certain as you prepare that you do not procrastinate. Someone has said that procrastination is the thief of time.

Actually, procrastination is much more. It is the thief of our self-respect. It nags at us and spoils our fun. It deprives us of the fullest realization of our ambitions and our hopes.

THE DECADE OF DECISIONS
Elder Robert D. Hales

Whenever we use our agency, we are either choosing to move toward a new door with many possibilities or into a closed corner with very few options. If we do what is right, our opportunities increase. If we don't, our opportunities decrease.

You, my friends, are in the critical period I call the decade of decisions. You must make many choices regarding education, employment, temple, missions, friends, dating, marriage, serving in the Church, and your family. As you choose, are your options and possibilities growing? Are you making the right choices? Is your future becoming brighter each day or are the lights dimming?

All of us should carefully consider what Heavenly Father wants us to do and how He may be preparing us. We should avoid trying to obtain the praise of the world and the honors of men.

When I was a little boy, my mother used to call me by saying as she went through the house, "Ding-ding, ding-ding. Calling

The very details of our lives are of interest to God. He cares about all of it—words, works, even thoughts. His interest and love are infinite in this way, and He will respond to our hopes and pleadings and help us in everything, including matters that seem unimportant or insignificant to others or even to ourselves.

—ELDER D. TODD CHRISTOFFERSON

Dr. Hales to surgery!" Being a doctor is a noble profession, but it wasn't right for me. I can't stand the sight of blood.

I caution all of us to avoid looking to the great and spacious building for answers to questions about our future pursuits, our companions, and our lifestyles. Instead, let us kneel and talk with our Heavenly Father, learn about our gifts and talents, find ways to develop them, make choices based on who we are and what we have been given, come to an understanding of what we are to accomplish here in mortality, and make the choices to bring it about.

THE POWER OF EDUCATION
President Russell M. Nelson

Wherever you are, develop a deep desire to learn. For us as Latter-day Saints, gaining an education is not just a privilege, it is a religious responsibility. "The glory of God is intelligence" (D&C 93:36). Indeed, our education is for the eternities.

Such a long-range perspective will help you make good choices about learning. I remember a conversation many years ago with a very bright sixteen-year-old high school student. He was uncertain about his religious commitment and undecided about his career. He wondered about the possibility of becoming a doctor of medicine. He asked me a simple question: "How many years did it take for you to become a heart surgeon?"

I quickly made the calculations: "From the time I graduated from high school until I first collected a fee for service as a surgeon, it took me fourteen years."

"Wow!" he replied. "That's too long for me!"

Then I asked, "How old will you be fourteen years from now if you don't become a heart surgeon?"

"Just the same," he replied. "Just the same!"

I had a special interest in this young man. On occasion I took him in my car on his early-morning route to deliver newspapers. Over the years his faith became strong. He was a powerful missionary. He decided to pursue his educational goal. First, he married his sweetheart in the temple. Then, while he studied medicine and surgery, they became the parents of four wonderful children. Now he is fully board certified as a heart surgeon–after intensive education and training over a period of fourteen years.

Brothers and sisters, don't be afraid to pursue your goals–even your dreams! There is no shortcut to excellence and competence. Education is the difference between *wishing* you could help other people and *being able* to help them.

While I was attending the university, I met Jon Huntsman, who would be my future employer and partner. He was my high council adviser while I was serving as elders quorum president.

After a year or so of knowing the Huntsmans, I was surprised one day when Jon invited me into his business office. I was a beginning senior at the university and just one year away from that long-sought-after degree in business. In that meeting Jon invited me to join his company in marketing and sales. I was overwhelmingly honored, and I felt that the deep and sincere prayer Sister Rasband and I had of finding meaningful employment was being answered.

I told Jon that I would be thrilled to join his company in the spring after graduation. I explained to him my quest for a college degree and how important it was to my family and me. Jon, in his very kind yet pointed way, explained that he needed me now. The next week he would be in Troy, Ohio, at one of his packaging plants to negotiate with a major customer. He told me if I wanted the job, I needed to be there to become their account manager. That was it—next week in Troy, Ohio, or no job offer at all!

That evening we prayed earnestly and sought the counsel of close loved ones and friends. The most important advice to me was from my sweet wife, Melanie: "Isn't this what people go to college for, to find an opportunity like this one?" The Spirit confirmed our decision, and I took the job in Ohio.

That week I walked off the campus of the University of Utah just two semesters short of receiving my degree. Eleven years later I was humbled when Jon Huntsman appointed me as the president of his global corporation with thousands of employees and billions in revenues. This should suggest that there is a masterpiece within each one of us, and when spiritually nurtured, carefully mentored, and loyally engaged in building up our families and the Lord's kingdom, all things are possible.

FAITH IN THE FUTURE
Elder Jeffrey R. Holland

When Sister Holland and I were married, we were as starstruck—and as fearful—as most of you are at these ages and stages of life. We had absolutely no money. Zero. We had an apartment just south of campus—the smallest we could find: two rooms and a half bath. We were both working too many hours trying to stay afloat financially, but we had no other choice.

I remember one fall day—I think it was in the first

semester after our marriage in 1963—we were walking together. Somewhere on that path we stopped and wondered what we had gotten ourselves into. Life that day seemed so overwhelming, and the undergraduate plus graduate years that we still anticipated before us seemed monumental, nearly insurmountable. Our love for each other and our commitment to the gospel were strong, but most of all the other temporal things around us seemed particularly ominous.

On a spot that I could probably still mark for you today, I turned to Pat and said something like this: "Honey, should we give up? I can get a good job and carve out a good living for us. I can do some things. I'll be okay without a degree. Should we stop trying to tackle what right now seems so difficult to face?"

Then my beloved little bride did what she has done for more than fifty years since then. She grabbed me by the lapels and said, "We are not going back. We are not going home. The future holds *everything* for us."

She stood there in the sunlight that day and gave me a real talk. I don't recall that she quoted the Apostle Paul, but there was certainly plenty in her voice that said she was committed to setting aside all that was past in order to "press toward the mark" (Philippians 3:14) and seize the prize of God that lay yet ahead. It was a living demonstration of faith. It was "the substance of things hoped for, the evidence of things not seen" (Hebrews 11:1). So we laughed, kept walking, and finished up sharing a root beer—one glass, two straws—at the then newly constructed Wilkinson Center.

Twenty years later I would, on occasion, look out of the window of the President's Home across the street from the Brimhall Building and picture there on the sidewalk two newlywed BYU students, down on their money and down even more on their confidence. And as I would gaze out that window, usually at night, I would occasionally see not Pat and Jeff Holland but you, walking that same sidewalk. I would see you sometimes as couples, sometimes as a group of friends, sometimes as just a lone student. I knew something of what you were feeling. Some of you were having thoughts such as these: Is there any future for me? What does a new year or a new semester or a new major or a new romance hold for me? Will I be safe? Will life be sound? Can I trust in the Lord and in the future? Or would it be better to look back, to go back, to go home?

To all such of every generation, I call out, faith is for the future. Faith builds on the past but never longs to stay there. Faith trusts that God has great things in store for each of us.

MARRIAGE

CHAPTER 6

A marriage partnership is not a crutch. You do not marry somebody you think is a little higher than the angels and then lean on him or her.

You develop your own gifts

*yourself and
and talents.*

As each partner develops,
you grow together, supporting
and strengthening one another.

—Elder Robert D. Hales

Opposition turns up almost anyplace something good has happened. It can happen when you are trying to get an education. It can hit you after your first month in your new mission field. It certainly happens in matters of love and marriage. I would like to have a dollar for every person in a courtship who knew he or she had felt the guidance of the Lord in that relationship, had prayed about the experience enough to know it was the will of the Lord, knew they loved each other and enjoyed each other's company, and saw a lifetime of wonderful compatibility ahead—only to panic, to get a brain cramp, to have total catatonic fear sweep over them. They "draw back," as Paul said (Hebrews 10:39), if not into perdition at least into marital paralysis.

I am not saying you shouldn't be very careful about something as significant and serious as marriage. And I certainly am not saying that a young man can get a revelation that he is to marry a certain person without that young woman getting the same confirmation. I have seen a lot of those one-way revelations in young people's lives. Yes, there are cautions and considerations to make, but once there has been genuine illumination, beware the temptation to retreat from a good thing. If it was right when you prayed about it and trusted it and lived for it, it is right now. Don't give up when the pressure mounts. You can find an apartment. You can win over your mother-in-law. You can sell your harmonica and therein fund one more meal. It's been done before. Don't give in. *Certainly don't give in to that being who is bent on the destruction of your happiness.* He wants everyone to be miserable like unto himself. Face your doubts. Master your fears. "Cast not away therefore your confidence" (Hebrews 10:35). Stay the course and see the beauty of life unfold for you.

CELESTIAL MARRIAGE
Elder Robert D. Hales

Temple marriage describes the place you go to have the marriage performed. *Celestial marriage* is being true to the sacred covenants you make in that temple marriage ceremony—living celestial principles in the marriage relationship.

A celestial marriage requires, after the vows are taken, a continuing consecrated life of worthiness leading to happiness and exaltation. If we live the laws properly, as they are intended, we will, with another individual and with our family, be able to have a little heaven on earth. We are practicing, when we live the laws pertaining to celestial marriage, the same laws that are practiced in heaven. We are practicing how to live with God the Father and His Son and with our families in the eternities to come. That to me is the message to the world of The Church of Jesus Christ of Latter-day Saints.

The aim of the gospel and the purpose of celestial marriage are not only to keep us together but also to make us eligible for our Heavenly Father's highest reward, exaltation in the celestial kingdom, increase in that kingdom, and being together with our families.

A SIGN BETWEEN US
President Thomas S. Monson

In a marriage, I would hope to learn the principle of acceptance. And I would learn that from President Hugh B. Brown, a man who for seven years said good-bye to his sweetheart each morning as she was confined to her bed, paralyzed from a stroke. And yet he was encouraged by her example. She would whisper good-bye; she would whisper hello; but that was about the extent of what Sister Brown could say. As I saw that loyal husband and father say good-bye to his wife and speak of her, I thought of the time when he and I came to Brigham Young University many years ago, when I was to give a commencement message. As we left President Brown's home and he entered the car, he said, "Before we leave, wait a moment." He took from his pocket a handkerchief, and he waved it out the window of the car. I looked toward the home and saw Sister Brown, sitting in a wheelchair in front of the window, waving her handkerchief back. He said, "Now we can go."

I said, "No, President Brown, I want to know what's all this about the waving of the handkerchief?"

He said, "From the first day we were married, when I heard a rap at the window as I walked down the pathway and turned and saw Sister Brown waving a handkerchief, I fumbled around and found one and waved back, and that has been a sign between the two of us that everything would be all right until we were together again that evening." What a beautiful lesson from which I might learn an important principle in life.

MOVE FORWARD WITH CONFIDENCE
Elder Quentin L. Cook

Commit yourself to the eternal institution of the family as the foundation for happiness. In the world at large, many are choosing not to get married or are delaying marriage. The family is an eternal institution ordained of God from before the foundation of the world. Most of you will marry and be blessed with the opportunity of having children. There is no greater blessing in this life than having children. Some of the most poignant passages in all of scripture capture the sublime significance of children in our Heavenly Father's plan. They are truly an heritage of the Lord (see Psalm 127:3).

When I was still in my twenties, President David O. McKay gave a prophetic message about marriage and children. He was ninety-five years old and in the last year of his life. He taught that the pure love between a man and a woman "is one of the noblest things on earth, and the bearing and rearing of children the highest of all human duties" (in Conference Report, April 1969, 15).

Let me assure you that the vast majority of marriages between faithful members of the Church are happy and successful. For those of you not yet married, you should move forward with faith and confidence to the ultimate goal of marriage and family. I would counsel you to find a righteous spouse that you admire and who will be your best friend. I assure you that the joy, love, and fulfillment experienced in loving, righteous families produces the greatest possible happiness we can achieve. It is also the foundation for a successful society.

I have sat in a number of meetings, in councils and com-mittees, where we have discussed the prevalent fear of entering into marriage and starting a family. Many of you are worried about the economic and political climate we live in. You're wait-ing to finish school, or pay off debt, or buy a home, or establish your career before getting married and starting a family. For some, it is fear that marital bliss may not be so blissful, or even worse that it could end in a divorce. Let me offer my perspective on these feelings.

Satan understands that the family is central to the Lord's plan of happiness. His strategy is to cast shadows of skepticism in your life. He is striving to sow the dark seeds of fear in your heart, anything to keep you from experiencing the most glori-ous, rewarding part of mortality: the bright holiness and happi-ness that comes from finding an eternal partner and bringing Heavenly Father's children into this world.

As you face the decision to start your own eternal family, do not wait because you are afraid. Remember the scripture, "be not afraid, only believe" (Mark 5:36). My marriage and family are a literal personal manifestation of the great plan of happiness for me. I promise you that the same can be true for you. Focusing the joyous light family life brings will cast out fear.

WHAT MAKES A GOOD MARRIAGE?
Elder Robert D. Hales

For those who are not now married, as you prepare for a temple marriage, there is great value in thinking about what makes a good marriage and the kind of person who will be able to make and keep temple covenants. Thinking ahead this way is why successful couples have been able to date and learn to know each other and come to know where the heart of that future companion will be for time and all eternity.

First, these successful couples know individually who they are—a son or daughter of God. They set eternal goals to once again live with our Heavenly Father and His Son Jesus Christ. They strive to leave the ways of the natural man behind.

Second, they know the doctrine and the importance of the saving temple ordinances and temple covenants and their necessity in achieving eternal goals.

Third, they choose to obtain the eternal blessings of the kingdom of God rather than the temporal or temporary possessions of the world.

Fourth, couples realize that when they are sealed for time

The family is not just the basic unit of society; it is the basic unit of eternity.

—ELDER M. RUSSELL BALLARD

and all eternity, they have chosen an eternal companion–their courting days are over! There is no need to look any further!

Fifth, couples think of one another before self. Selfishness suffocates spiritual senses. Remember that. Communicating with the Lord in prayer, they grow together and not apart. They converse with each other, thereby never letting little things become big things. They talk early about the "little hurts" with little fear of offending. In this way, when the pressure in the tea kettle builds and the whistle goes off, there is no explosion of bitter feelings. They are willing to apologize and ask forgiveness if they have hurt the one they love. They express their love for each other and become closer. They lift and strengthen one another.

THE POWER OF PARTNERSHIP
President Russell M. Nelson

There is great power in a strong partnership. True partners can achieve more than the sum of each acting alone. With true partners, one plus one is much more than two. For example, Dr. Will Mayo and his brother, Dr. Charles Mayo, formed the Mayo Clinic. Lawyers and others form important partnerships. And in marriage, a husband and wife can form the most significant partnership of all–an eternal family.

Sustainable improvements in any endeavor depend on

collaboration and agreement. Great leaders and partners develop the skill of sharing insights and efforts and the pattern of building consensus. Great partners are completely loyal. They suppress personal ego in exchange for being part of creating something larger than themselves. Great partnerships are dependent upon each individual developing his or her own personal attributes of character.

Male and female are created for what they can do and become, together. It takes a man and a woman to bring a child into the world. Mothers and fathers are not interchangeable. Men and women are distinct and complementary. Children deserve a chance to grow up with both a mom and a dad.

FINDING AN ETERNAL COMPANION
President Thomas S. Monson

Many years ago I served as a mission president. When we returned home to Salt Lake City after three years, my dear wife and I were a little surprised one evening as we ran a tally on our missionaries, only to find that there were some sister missionaries who had not as yet found an eternal companion. We determined we would do what we could to help out.

I said to Sister Monson, "Frances, let's plan with a purpose and invite three or four of our lovely sister missionaries to our home. We'll have an activity where they can tell us who of all the single returned male missionaries they would like to have invited to a little fireside in our home. Then we will show pictures of the mission, and we will arrange the seating so that they can become well acquainted with one another."

This was done, and I might say that the four girls whom we invited eagerly responded to the challenge. In shoe boxes we maintained individual five-by-seven-inch photographs of every missionary. We had four such boxes, with missionary pictures in each. As those four girls sat around our living room, I said to each of them, "Here is a gift. Thumb through your box of pictures and tell me which of all the pictures represents the young man whom you would most like to have invited to come to this fireside." My, that was an interesting scene. I think that the only way I could adequately describe it is to ask a question. Have you ever seen children on Christmas morning?

We went forward and invited the chosen four young men to join these four young ladies in our home, and we had a glorious evening. At the conclusion of the evening, I noticed two of them slowly walking down our driveway, and I said to Sister Monson, "This looks promising."

It wasn't long afterward that I received a telephone call

from the young man. He said, "President Monson, do you remember that I promised you if I ever fell in love, I would let you know?"

I said, "Yes, sir."

He continued, "President, I have fallen in love."

I replied, "Good. With whom?"

He said, "You'll never guess."

I was discreet; I didn't guess. I said, "You tell me."

And he named the sister missionary with whom he walked side by side and hand in hand from our party that evening. They have now been married for more than fifty years and have five children and many grandchildren.

Some of you within the sound of my voice have already married; others are still seeking that special someone with whom you would want to spend eternity. For those of you in the latter category, in your quest for the man or woman of your dreams, you may well heed the counsel given by King Arthur in the musical *Camelot*. Faced with a particularly vexing dilemma, King Arthur could well have been speaking to all of us when he declared, "We must not let our passions destroy our dreams." May you follow this most essential counsel. I urge you to hold fast to your standards. I plead with you not to waver.

SERVICE

CHAPTER 7

Being outwardly directed, caring about others, and serving others increases our spiritual stability.

Eternity stays in we focus on others Heavenly Father's

clearer focus when as we seek to help children in some way.

I have always found it much easier to receive inspiration when I am praying to find out how I can help another than when I am simply praying for myself.

—Elder Dale G. Renlund

PREPARING FOR A LIFE OF SERVICE
Elder Robert D. Hales

To assist you in living lives of service, let me suggest three essential principles:

First, help others succeed.

In the world you will discover many people who seem to be average in their intelligence and yet are very, very successful. Why? Because they know that it is impossible to succeed alone. The only way to truly succeed is to help others succeed as well.

Second, learn and develop your own talents and value the talents of others.

After graduating from business school as a young man, I learned an essential lesson. A competitor company was taking away our loyal customers, and I was assigned the responsibility of developing a new product to safeguard our market share. This responsibility humbled me, to say the least. In preparing for this assignment, the chairman of the board said to me in a private conversation, "Bob, I have confidence in the abilities you have learned thus far. Now I want you to expand your vision and understanding. I want you to learn to think like a leader and see the whole picture!"

What was "the whole picture"? I soon realized it not only

included my own gifts and talents but also the gifts and talents of others. I had come from a marketing background and had fallen into the myopic mentality that my area of expertise was very important. Although marketing is necessary, I began learning the importance of all the other elements in the process: research, development, testing, manufacturing, and so forth.

Which part of the process is most important? The only right answer to that question is: None is most important because all are necessary. Or, to say it scripturally, "The eye cannot say unto the hand, I have no need of thee: nor again the head to the feet, I have no need of you" (1 Corinthians 12:21).

Third, obtain a spirit of serving and giving.

Let me remind you that your capacity to obtain and act upon this spirit of service and giving may depend upon your obedience to temporal commandments. The living prophets have counseled us time and again to put our lives in order—to pay a full tithing and a generous fast offering, to store food and other essential items, and to become self-sufficient by eliminating debt. Let us reap the blessings that will come from obedience to this counsel.

What are those blessings? In time, as you work hard and pay an honest tithe, you will be able to provide for your own needs and the needs of your family. Then you will have the privilege of acting upon the spirit of service and giving.

THINKING OF OTHERS FIRST
Elder Gary E. Stevenson

Think more about the welfare of others than you think about yourself. Martin Luther King Jr. noted, "On the parable of the Good Samaritan: I imagine that the first question the priest and Levite asked was 'If I stop to help this man, what will happen to me?' But by the very nature of his concern, the Good Samaritan reversed the question: 'If I do not stop to help this man, what will happen to him?'" (*Strength to Love* [1980]). Dr. King understood that service and selflessness could eradicate fear.

My wife demonstrated her understanding of this principle when she instituted what we called "Lesa's cookie therapy" while we were serving as mission presidents in Nagoya, Japan. Occasionally, we would have a missionary come to us who was struggling, often with doubt or fear, and ready to call it quits. Lesa would gather a few supplies, hand them to the missionary, and say, "Here's what I want you to do. Take these ingredients and make chocolate chip cookies every morning. Package them and deliver them to someone who needs them." This act of thinking about someone else rather than oneself often cured the missionary of his or her fears. The same is true for you. The warm, golden glow that accompanies service and selflessness has the power to melt away doubts and fears.

SERVANTS OF THE LORD
President Henry B. Eyring

The word *servant* is not an exalted title for most of us. The picture it brings to mind—probably from an old movie—is of you as a server standing behind people of higher social status than you. They are seated at a table, and the servant waits on them. The servant may be dressed beautifully and may even stand with head carried at a noble angle, but few of us would find ourselves pleased with the thought that our education had prepared us for what appears to be a demeaning place. Most of us have, at least unconsciously, seen ourselves as working for an education so that we might sit at the table of abundance—not become a servant of others.

But there is another way to see the word *servant.* When the Lord Jesus Christ wishes to dignify those He loves and trusts, He uses the title as praise: "My servant."

Your key and mine to rising to our potential as servants is to know our Master, to do for Him what we can, and be content to leave the residue in His hands. Let me give you an example that will face you in the days ahead. You will be torn between the demands to put bread on the table and a roof over your head, to take care of a family need, to respond to the cries of the widows or the orphans around you, and at the same time to meet the requirements of the calling you have accepted in the Church. When that happens, you will be sorely tempted to murmur, perhaps even to complain. But remember that you serve a Master who loves you, who knows you, and who is all-powerful. He has created not demands for your service but opportunities for your growth. You can pray to Him with confidence and ask, "What would you have me do next?"

If you listen humbly and with faith, you will feel an answer. And you will, if you are wise and good, set about to do that which your Master has commanded. And you will leave the residue in His hands. As His servant I promise you that you will find that some of those residual tasks you left will be done when you return to them. Others will have been prepared for you. And you will be the stronger for the task you already tackled. Then, when you pray again, an answer will come again. And you will move on to the next task, at peace and not complaining.

START SERVING NOW
Elder Dale G. Renlund

We may believe that at some future point we will be in a better situation to help our fellowman. In reality, now is the time. Having this "fiber" of service become part of who we are is not situational. We are sorely mistaken if we think that at some future point it will be more convenient when we have more time, more money, or more anything to serve others better. Now is the time to begin. Our spiritual stability will instantly improve.

My father taught my brother, sisters, and me that helping others is a duty, a choice that we make regardless of our own circumstances. My dad was born in northern Finland, outside the town of Jakobstad, which is also known as Pietasaari. He loved Finnish literature, especially the works of a Finnish poet, Johan Ludvig Runeberg. Runeberg had also been born in Jakobstad.

One of Runeberg's poems that we heard over and over told the story of Farmer Paavo. Paavo was a poor peasant farmer who lived with his wife and children in Saarijärvi in the lake region of central Finland. Several years in a row, some combination of the runoff from the spring snowmelt, summer hailstorms, or an early autumn frost killed most of his crop.

Each time the meager harvest came in, his wife said, "Paavo, Paavo, you unfortunate old man. God has forsaken us."

Paavo, in turn, said, "Woman, mix bark with the rye flour to make bread so we won't go hungry. I will work harder to drain the marshy fields. God is testing us, but He will provide."

Every time the crop was destroyed, Paavo directed his wife to double the amount of bark that she mixed into the bread to ward off starvation. Poor Paavo worked even harder. He dug ditches to drain the marsh to decrease his fields' susceptibility to the spring snowmelt and to the exposure of an early frost.

Finally, Paavo harvested a rich crop. Overjoyed, his wife said, "Paavo, Paavo, these are happy times! It is time to throw away the bark and bake bread made only with the rye."

But Paavo took his wife's hand and said, "Woman, mix the bread with half bark, for our neighbor's fields have frosted over" (Johan Ludvig Runeberg, "Högt Bland Saarijärvis Moar" ["High Among Saarijärvi Moor"], see sv.wikisource.org/wiki/författare :Johan_Ludvig_Runeberg. The translation from Runeberg's original is mine).

Left unstated in the poem was Paavo's intent to help his devastated, destitute neighbor.

As I have reread that story as an adult, I have come to understand a little bit better what my dad was trying to teach me and my siblings. Regardless of circumstances, we have a choice. Will we help others or not? We flunk a significant test of mortality if we do not choose to help those in need. And, if we do help, we increase our own spiritual stability. Serving others allows us to express that fiber of which an exalted life in the celestial kingdom is made.

Be involved in the world
in a positive way and be a
powerful force for good.

—ELDER QUENTIN L. COOK

A MULTITUDE OF OPPORTUNITIES
President Henry B. Eyring

Vibrant faith in God comes best from serving Him regularly. Not all of us have received callings to offices in the Church. Some of you may not yet be called to something in a formal way, yet every member has a multitude of opportunities to serve God.

Most of us have or may have callings as home and visiting teachers. There is in those callings great opportunity to grow in faith that the Lord sends the Holy Ghost to His humble servants. That builds faith and renews our faith in Him. I've seen it and so have many of you. I received a phone call from a distraught mother in a state far away from where I was. She told me that her unmarried daughter had moved to another city far from her home. She sensed from the little contact she had with her daughter that something was terribly wrong. The mother feared for the moral safety of her daughter. She pleaded with me to help her daughter.

I found out who the daughter's home teacher was. I called him. He was young. And yet he and his companion both had been awakened in the night with not only concern for the girl but with inspiration that she was about to make choices that would bring sadness and misery. With only the inspiration of the Spirit, they went to see her. She did not at first want to tell them anything about her situation. They pleaded with her to repent and to choose to follow the path that the Lord had set out for her and that her mother and father had taught her to follow. She realized as she listened that the only way they could have known what they knew about her life was from God. A mother's prayer had gone to Heavenly Father, and the Holy Ghost had been sent to home teachers with an errand.

More than once I have heard priesthood leaders say that they had been inspired to go to someone in need, only to find the visiting teacher or the home teacher had already been there. My wife is an example. We had a bishop once who said to me, "You know, it bothers me—when I get an inspiration to go to someone, your wife has already been there." Your faith will grow as you serve the Lord in caring for Heavenly Father's children as the Lord's teacher to their home. You will have your prayers answered. You will come to know for yourself that He lives, that He loves us, and that He sends inspiration to those with even the beginnings of faith in Him and with the desire to serve Him in His Church.

Seek heavenly help to know how to serve others. There is no feeling so gratifying nor knowledge so comforting as knowing that our Father has answered the prayer of another through you.

May I share with you an experience I had with a dear friend of mine, Louis McDonald. Louis never married. Because of a crippling disease, he had never known a day without pain nor many days without loneliness. One winter's day, as I visited him, he was slow in answering the doorbell's ring. I entered his well-kept home; the temperature in save but one room—the kitchen—was a chilly 40 degrees. The reason? Insufficient money to heat any other room. The walls needed papering, the ceilings needed to be lowered, the cupboards needed to be filled.

I was troubled by Louis's needs. A bishop was consulted, and a miracle of love, prompted by testimony, took place. The members of the ward—particularly the young single adults—were organized and the labor of love begun.

A month later, my friend Louis called and asked if I would come and see what had happened to him. I did and indeed beheld a miracle. The sidewalks, which had been uprooted by large poplar trees, had been replaced, the porch of the home rebuilt, a new door with glistening hardware installed, the ceilings lowered, the walls papered, the woodwork painted, the roof replaced, and the cupboards filled. No longer was the home chilly and uninviting. It now seemed to whisper a warm welcome.

Louis saved until last showing me his pride and joy: there on his bed was a beautiful plaid quilt bearing the crest of his McDonald family clan. It had been made with loving care by the women of the Relief Society. Before leaving, I discovered that each week the young single adults would bring in a hot dinner and share a home evening. Warmth had replaced the cold, repairs had transformed the wear of years, but, more significantly, hope had dispelled despair, and now love reigned triumphant.

As we go about our daily lives, we discover countless opportunities to follow the example of the Savior. When our hearts are in tune with His teachings, we discover the unmistakable nearness of His divine help. We are on the Lord's errand, and when we are on the Lord's errand, we are entitled to the Lord's help.

CHALLENGES
OF YOUR DAY

Prophets see ahead. They see the harrowing dangers the adversary has placed or will yet place in our path.

Prophets also possibilities and those who listen with

foresee the grand privileges awaiting the intent to obey.

I know this is true! I have experienced it for myself over and over again.

—President Russell M. Nelson

PUTTING THE SAVIOR FIRST
Elder D. Todd Christofferson

The cost of joining the Church of Jesus Christ can be very high, but the admonition to prefer Christ above all others, even our closest family members, applies also to those who may have been born in the covenant. Many of us became members of the Church without opposition, perhaps as children. The challenge we may confront is remaining loyal to the Savior and His Church in the face of parents, in-laws, brothers or sisters, or even our children whose conduct, beliefs, or choices make it impossible to support both Him and them. It is not a question of love. We can and must love one another as Jesus loves us. As He said, "By this shall all men know that ye are my disciples, if ye have love one to another" (John 13:35). But, the Lord reminds us, "He that loveth father or mother more than me is not worthy of me: and he that loveth son or daughter more than me is not worthy of me" (Matthew 10:37). So although familial love continues, relationships may be interrupted and, according to the circumstances, even support or tolerance at times suspended for the sake of our higher love.

In reality, the best way to help those we love—the best way to love them—is to continue to put the Savior first. If we cast ourselves adrift from the Lord out of sympathy for loved ones who are suffering or distressed, then we lose the means by which we might have helped them. If, however, we remain firmly rooted in faith in Christ, we are in a position both to receive and to offer divine help. If (or I should say when) the moment comes that a beloved family member wants desperately to turn to the only true and lasting source of help, he or she will know whom to trust as a guide and a companion. In the meantime, with the gift of the Holy Spirit to guide, we can perform a steady ministry to lessen the pain of poor choices and bind up the wounds insofar as we are permitted. Otherwise, we serve neither those we love nor ourselves.

THE COUNSEL OF PROPHETS
President Russell M. Nelson

The First Presidency and Quorum of the Twelve Apostles counsel together and share all the Lord has directed us to understand and to feel individually and collectively. And then we watch the Lord move upon the President of the Church to proclaim the Lord's will.

This prophetic process was followed in 2012 with the change in minimum age for missionaries and again with the recent additions to the Church's handbook, consequent to the legalization of same-sex marriage in some countries. Filled with compassion for all, and especially for the children, we wrestled at length to understand the Lord's will in this matter. Ever mindful of God's plan of salvation and of His hope for eternal life for each of His children, we considered countless permutations and combinations of possible scenarios that could arise. We met repeatedly in the temple in fasting and prayer and sought further direction and inspiration. And then, when the Lord inspired His prophet, President Thomas S. Monson, to declare the mind of the Lord and the will of the Lord, each of us during that sacred moment felt a spiritual confirmation. It was our privilege as Apostles to sustain what had been revealed to President Monson. Revelation from the Lord to His servants is a sacred process, and so is your privilege of receiving personal revelation.

You may not always understand every declaration of a living prophet. But when you know a prophet is a prophet, you can approach the Lord in humility and faith and ask for your own witness about whatever His prophet has proclaimed.

Around 41 B.C., many Nephites joined the Church, and the Church prospered. But secret combinations also began to grow, and many of their cunning leaders hid among the people and were difficult to detect. As the people became more and more prideful, many of the Nephites made "a mock of that which was sacred, denying the spirit of prophecy and of revelation" (Helaman 4:12).

Those same threats are among us today. The somber reality is that there are "servants of Satan" (D&C 10:5) embedded throughout society. So be very careful about whose counsel you follow.

SAME-SEX MARRIAGE
Elder M. Russell Ballard

Apostles are charged to be watchmen on the towers to see and teach the doctrines of Christ. All of you know that the traditional definition of marriage is under attack today. There are those who are framing the discussion focused in terms of civil rights. The First Presidency and the Quorum of the Twelve Apostles explained the Church's position and doctrine of God's purpose and plan for His spirit children to experience mortal life, which is essential to our everlasting and eternal life.

I would suppose many of you may not have read the statement that was issued on this subject. I quote from this statement and ask you to pay careful attention to the words:

"Changes in the civil law do not, indeed cannot, change the moral law that God has established. God expects us to uphold and keep His commandments regardless of divergent opinions or trends in society. His law of chastity is clear: sexual relations are proper only between a man and a woman who are legally and lawfully wedded as husband and wife. We urge you to review and teach Church members the doctrine contained in 'The Family: A Proclamation to the World.'"

The statement continues:

"Just as those who promote same-sex marriage are entitled to civility, the same is true for those who oppose it. . . .

"As members of the Church, we are responsible to teach the gospel of Jesus Christ and to illuminate the great blessings that flow from heeding God's commandments as well as the inevitable consequences of ignoring them. We invite you to pray that people everywhere will have their hearts softened to the truths of the gospel, and that wisdom will be granted to those who are called upon to decide issues critical to society's future" (Letter from the First Presidency of The Church of Jesus Christ of Latter-day Saints, dated Jan. 10, 2014 [United States] and Mar. 6, 2014 [outside the United States]; https://www.lds.org/church /news/lds-church-instructs-leaders-regarding-same-sex -marriage).

I know you love and support the Lord and sustain His

prophets, but I also know that some of you may be confused on the many implications of the Church's decision to sustain God's revealed plan for His children.

I also know that some of our youth struggle to understand how to explain the doctrine surrounding family and marriage and still remain kind, gentle, and loving toward those who do not agree. You may be afraid that you will be labeled as a bigot and as being intolerant.

You may know someone who struggles with same-sex attraction or has made a decision to live in a same-gender relationship. Your love for that person as a son or daughter of God can create an inward struggle as you try to love and support him or her and still stand for the Lord's eternal plan of happiness.

Let us be clear–The Church of Jesus Christ of Latter-day Saints believes that "the experience of same-sex attraction is a complex reality for many people. The attraction itself is not a sin, but acting on it is. Even though individuals do not choose to have such attractions, they do choose how to respond to them. With love and understanding, the Church reaches out to all God's children, including [those with same-sex attraction]" ("Love One Another: A Discussion on Same-Sex Attraction," mormonsandgays.org).

The Church does not teach or advocate shunning or other unchristianlike actions. We must love and strive to help others to understand that no one should ignore or discount the commandments of God.

DISCRIMINATION
Elder Ronald A. Rasband

I am going to tell you the stories of two people who may be just a little older than you, and, as I do so, I would like you to think about how you would feel if you were one of these individuals.

The first story is about someone I will call Ethan. He had recently started his job in a career he had longed for, and he wanted to make a good impression. He came early to work and stayed late. He picked up extra projects and did excellent work. He was well liked by many of his colleagues and was enjoying his job. One day at lunch with a couple of coworkers he felt comfortable telling them that he was gay. An awkward silence developed because no one knew how to respond and the work environment was quite conservative. Ethan was disappointed by their cold response and felt hurt and rejected. He began to feel vulnerable at work and less valued.

After that lunch meeting, things became increasingly awkward for Ethan at work. He found himself excluded from

Cynicism is an intellectual cop-out, a crutch for a withered soul, a thin excuse for inaction and retreating commitment. Do not become cynical; be appropriately concerned and actively involved.

—ELDER JEFFREY R. HOLLAND

large projects and social activities after work, and his productivity began to suffer, as he felt he did not belong and was not wanted. After a few months he was let go because his boss felt he was not keeping up. Despite all the claims to the contrary, Ethan knew he had been fired for being gay.

Now I want to tell you about Samantha. Samantha had just started work in the administrative offices of a local university. She was excited to work in a stimulating environment full of diverse thoughts, ideas, and backgrounds. One day at work a coworker approached Samantha and said she had heard that Samantha was a Mormon and asked if that was true. Samantha cheerfully responded that it was, but the question that followed brought her up short.

"So why do you hate gays?" her coworker asked. Samantha was surprised by the question but tried to explain her belief in God and God's plan for His children, which she believed included guidelines on moral and sexual behavior. Her coworker countered by telling her that the rest of society had progressed beyond those beliefs. "And besides," she said, "history is full of people using religious teachings to wage wars and marginalize vulnerable groups."

Samantha restated her convictions and her understanding

of God's love for all people and then asked for her coworker to respect her right to believe. The coworker felt compelled to tell other employees about their conversation, and over the next few weeks Samantha felt increasingly isolated as more and more coworkers confronted her with questions and attacks.

Samantha's boss, seeing the increase in religious conversations in the workplace, cautioned Samantha against proselytizing in their work environment or her job would be in jeopardy. Her work, like Ethan's, began to suffer. Rather than risk being fired, Samantha started to look for another job.

Now, these are hypothetical stories, and yet they are not. There are many Samanthas and Ethans. However we choose to live and whatever choices we make, we all share a common humanity and desire for fairness and kindness. Ethan should not have been fired for being gay and Samantha should not have been intimidated for being religious. Both were wrongly criticized, judged, and retaliated against.

In today's society it is politically correct to empathize with Ethan's situation but less so with Samantha's. Ethan may find his case picked up by an advocacy group as yet another example of anti-gay discrimination. And, indeed, he does deserve protection.

But what about Samantha? Who will defend her right to religious conscience? What about her right to live authentically as a person of faith, committed to loving and serving everyone but also with the right to choose what is right and wrong and to live her life accordingly?

CONFRONTING PORNOGRAPHY
Elder M. Russell Ballard

More than 180 years ago, the Lord revealed His law of health, including a warning about the use of tobacco (see D&C 89). Millions of people listened to the Lord, but many more did not. No one knew at that time or even when I was your age the long-term effects of smoking. Today, after decades of scientific research, we now know smoking's effect on lung cancer and other deadly diseases. The Lord's Word of Wisdom was a protective blessing.

In similar ways the Lord in our day has warned us about the effects of pornography. Millions of people faithfully follow the Lord's counsel, whereas countless others do not. We don't have to wait, my dear friends, for 180 or even for ten years to discover the devastating effects of pornography because current scientific research has revealed that pornography cripples young adults in several ways and poisons their chances of one day having a loving and lasting marriage relationship.

Research has also shown that frequent use of pornography can lead to obsessive behaviors and can rewire the brain to capture a person in the prison of addiction.

Research has also verified that pornography fosters unrealistic expectations and delivers dangerous miseducation about healthy human intimacy.

Most insidiously, pornography conditions you to see people as objects that you can disregard and disrespect both emotionally and physically.

Another aspect of pornography is that it is generally a "secret" activity. Users often hide their use or at least minimize their use from everyone, including their romantic partners and spouses. Studies have found that when people engage in this type of self-concealment–when they do things they are not proud of and keep those things a secret from their family members and friends–it not only hurts their relationships and leaves them feeling lonely but also makes them more vulnerable to depression, anxiety, and poor self-esteem. Keeping secrets damages trust.

Initially, we must avoid pornography ourselves because it is deadly. It kills genuine, tender human relationships–destroying marriages and families. It destroys the spirit of the person who consumes it as surely as the most deadly poison kills the body and the mind.

My dear young brothers and sisters, do not be deceived. Do not think that once you go on your mission or once you get married you can stop this addictive behavior. If you are involved in it now, if you are entrapped in this practice, get spiritual help now. You can overcome pornography with the Savior's assistance. Do not wait! I plead with you to leave it alone! There are many resources on LDS.org that will override the darkness of pornographic images.

These are challenging days—but no more challenging than the days of Helaman and his stripling warriors when they stood to defend their families and the Church. This is your time to step forward and join the ranks of other righteous and dedicated young men and young women to fight the battle against pornography.

BASIC MORALITY
Elder Quentin L. Cook

Some of you may have succumbed to conduct that goes well beyond just fun and games. Those involved with pornography or any other form of immorality are acting out a different role from what they really want to be or should be. It is interesting that almost everyone who is involved with pornography assumes a false identity and hides his or her participation. They mask their conduct, which they know is reprehensible and destructive to everyone they care about. Pornography is a plague that is detrimental not only to a person's moral standing with God, but it can also destroy marriages and families and has an adverse impact on society. Pornography and sexual immorality aside, there are other insidious behaviors that poison society and undermine basic morality. The Apostle Paul wrote: "Be not deceived: evil communications corrupt good manners. Awake to righteousness, and sin not; for some have not the knowledge of God" (1 Corinthians 15:33-34).

It is clear that evil communications are not just a matter of bad manners, but, if practiced by those who are Latter-day Saints, they can adversely affect those who do not have knowledge of God or a testimony of the Savior.

Any use of the Internet to bully, destroy a reputation, or place a person in a bad light is reprehensible. What we are seeing in society is that when people wear the mask of anonymity, they are more likely to engage in this kind of conduct, which is so destructive of civil discourse. It also violates the basic principles the Savior taught.

RELIGIOUS FREEDOM

The opportunity to be involved in the political process is a privilege given to every citizen.

Our laws and an important teaching our social and

legislation play role in shaping moral culture.

We need every individual in society to take an active role in engaging in civic dialogue that helps frame laws and legislation that are fair for everyone.

—Elder Ronald A. Rasband

GOVERNMENT AND RELIGION
Elder Dallin H. Oaks

The free "exercise" of religion obviously involves both the right to choose religious beliefs and affiliations and the right to "exercise" or practice those beliefs. But in a nation with citizens of many different religious beliefs, the right of some to act upon their religious principles must be qualified by the government's responsibility to protect the health and safety of all. Otherwise, for example, the government could not protect its citizens' person or property from neighbors whose intentions include taking human life or stealing in circumstances rationalized on the basis of their religious beliefs.

Unpopular minority religions are especially dependent upon a constitutional guarantee of free exercise of religion. We are fortunate to have such a guarantee in the United States, but many nations do not. The importance of that guarantee in the United States should make us ever diligent to defend it. And it is in need of being defended. During my lifetime I have seen a significant deterioration in the respect accorded to religion in our public life, and I believe that the vitality of religious freedom is in danger of being weakened accordingly.

I offer some points of counsel on how Latter-day Saints

should conduct themselves to enhance religious freedom in this period of turmoil and challenge.

First, we must speak with love, always showing patience, understanding, and compassion toward our adversaries.

Second, we must not be deterred or coerced into silence by intimidation. We must insist on our constitutional right and duty to exercise our religion, to vote our consciences on public issues, and to participate in elections and debates in the public square and the halls of justice. These are the rights of all citizens and they are also the rights of religious leaders. While our church rarely speaks on public issues, it does so by exception on what the First Presidency defines as significant moral issues, which could surely include laws affecting the fundamental legal/cultural/moral environment of our communities and nations.

We must also insist on this companion condition of democratic government: when churches and their members or any other group act or speak out on public issues, win or lose, they have a right to expect freedom from retaliation.

Third, we must insist on our freedom to preach the doctrines of our faith. Why do I make this obvious point? Religious people who share our moral convictions feel some intimidation.

Fortunately, our leaders do not refrain from stating and explaining our position.

We will continue to teach what our Heavenly Father has commanded us to teach, and trust that the precious free exercise of religion remains strong enough to guarantee our right to exercise this most basic freedom.

THE FULNESS OF THE RESTORATION
President Dieter F. Uchtdorf

The Restoration in its fulness completes and enhances the truths found in the religions of the world. Latter-day Saints are occasionally accused of being narrow-minded or unwilling to consider the beliefs of others. Such accusations may be true of Latter-day Saints who do not understand their own religion, but those who know the position of the Church regarding the beliefs of other people willingly allow all to "worship how, where, or what they may" (Articles of Faith 1:11).

Having the fulness of the gospel should not lead any of us to feel arrogant or harbor a holier-than-thou attitude. We should simply be grateful with all our heart for the truth restored and for the privilege of bringing this truth and these eternal blessings to our brothers and sisters.

Brothers and sisters, let us never be ashamed to testify of this wonderful Restoration, the restored gospel of Jesus Christ, "for it is the power of God unto salvation to every one that believeth" (Romans 1:16).

Let us never be ashamed to testify that Joseph Smith was a true prophet of God and that we have a living prophet today.

The keys of the kingdom of God have been restored again, and they are held by Apostles of the Lord Jesus Christ. The President of The Church of Jesus Christ of Latter-day Saints, who is the senior Apostle, holds all the keys necessary to preside over all the organizational and ordinance work of the Church. He stands as the prophet of God—the most recent in an unbroken succession of prophets and apostles from Joseph Smith to our own day. This is my apostolic witness of the reality of the Restoration and the truthfulness of this great work.

CIVIC INVOLVEMENT
Elder Quentin L. Cook

In addition to personal attributes, qualities, and decisions, if you are to be the generation you need to be, you will build your country and the community where you live. Your generation, like the Greatest Generation, will need to protect righteousness and religious freedom. The Judeo-Christian heritage we have inherited is not only precious but also essential to our Father in Heaven's plan. We need to preserve it for future generations. We need to join with good people, including those of all faiths–especially those who feel accountable to God for their conduct. The successful enhancement of Judeo-Christian values and religious freedom will mark your generation as the great generation it needs to be.

With the challenges that exist in the world today, the First Presidency and Quorum of the Twelve are particularly concerned that you participate appropriately in the political process in the country where you live. The Church is neutral in political contests and does not support candidates or parties. We do expect, however, that our members will be fully engaged in supporting the candidates and parties of their choice based on principles that will protect good government. Our doctrine is clear: those who are "honest . . . and wise . . . should be sought for diligently" (D&C 98:10). "When the wicked rule the people mourn" (D&C 98:9). This means that everyone should feel obligated to vote.

We would hope this would be true of all citizens, members and nonmembers alike, in all states and all countries where elections are held. The price of freedom has been too high, and the consequences of nonparticipation are too great for any citizens to feel they can ignore their responsibility.

TOLERANCE
Elder Dallin H. Oaks

Tolerance is defined as a friendly and fair attitude toward unfamiliar opinions and practices or toward the persons who hold or practice them. As modern transportation and communication have brought all of us into closer proximity to different peoples and different ideas, we have greater need for tolerance.

This greater exposure to diversity both enriches our lives and complicates them. We are enriched by associations with different peoples, which remind us of the wonderful diversity of the children of God. But diversities in cultures and values also challenge us to identify what can be embraced as consistent with our gospel culture and values and what cannot. In this way diversity increases the potential for conflict and requires us to be more thoughtful about the nature of tolerance. What is tolerance, when does it apply, and when does it not apply?

This is a harder question for those who affirm the existence of God and absolute truth than for those who believe in moral relativism. The weaker one's belief in God and the fewer one's moral absolutes, the fewer the occasions when the ideas or practices of others will confront one with the challenge to be tolerant. For example, an atheist has no need to decide what kinds and occasions of profanity or blasphemy can be tolerated and what kinds should be confronted. Persons who don't believe in God or in absolute truth in moral matters can see themselves as the most tolerant of persons. For them, almost anything goes. "You do your thing, and I'll do my thing" is the popular description. This belief system can tolerate almost any behavior and almost any persons. Unfortunately, some who believe in moral relativism seem to have difficulty tolerating those who insist that there is a God who should be respected and certain moral absolutes that should be observed.

Living together with mutual respect for one another's differences is a challenge in today's world. However–this living with differences is what the gospel of Jesus Christ teaches us we must do.

The kingdom of God is like a leaven, Jesus taught (see Matthew 13:33). A leaven–yeast–is hidden away in the larger mass until the whole is leavened, which means raised by its influence.

Since followers of Jesus Christ are commanded to be a leaven–not to be taken out of the world, but to remain in it–we

The religion into which a person is born may be incomplete, but it can still serve as a foundation for the reception of the fulness of the gospel. We are wise when we show respect for the beliefs of others.

—PRESIDENT DIETER F. UCHTDORF

must seek tolerance from those who hate us for not being of the world. As part of this, we will sometimes need to challenge laws that would impair our freedom to practice our faith, doing so in reliance on our constitutional rights to the free exercise of religion. That is why we need understanding and support–including *your* understanding and support–when we must contend for religious freedom.

Our tolerance and respect for others and their beliefs does not cause us to abandon our commitment to the truths we understand and the covenants we have made. We are cast as combatants in the war between truth and error. There is no middle ground. We must stand up for truth, even while we practice tolerance and respect for beliefs and ideas different from our own and for the people who hold them.

A MESSAGE OF FAIRNESS
Elder Ronald A. Rasband

I would like to talk with you about three things you can do–each one of you–to support and promote a message of fairness.

First, try to view others through a lens of fairness. To do this requires you to first acknowledge that Heavenly Father loves all of His children equally. He has said, "Love one another;

as I have loved you" (John 13:34). There is no choice, sin, or mistake that you or anyone else can make that will change His love for you or for them. That does not mean He excuses or condones sinful conduct; nor do we, in ourselves or in others. But that does mean we reach out in love to persuade, to help, and to rescue.

Second, let fairness guide your treatment of others. Jesus Christ looked past people's ethnicity, rank, and circumstances in order to teach them simple truth. Remember the Samaritan woman at the well, the Roman centurion, and the unpopular publican. The Lord has commanded us to follow His example, saying, "Ye shall observe to do the things which ye have seen me do" (JST, Matthew 26:25). Do not judge people or treat them unfairly because they sin differently than you, or we, do.

Perhaps the greatest challenge in treating others fairly is in the balance required in supporting religious freedom when you have friends or family members who experience same-sex attraction or who are firm supporters of their rights. Some of you worry that you will appear intolerant or unsupportive if you seek protections to exercise your faith publicly and freely.

Again, study the life of our Savior and seek His guidance. The Savior demonstrated perfectly how to reach out in love and encouragement while also holding firm to what we know to be true. Remember that when the woman was caught in adultery, the Lord asked for anyone without sin to step forward and be the first to condemn her. When no one approached, our Savior, who was without sin, commented, "Neither do I condemn thee: go, and sin no more" (John 8:11). The forgiveness and kindness He showed her did not contradict His teachings that sexual intimacy is meant for a husband and a wife who are legally and lawfully married. You too can be unyielding in right and truth yet still reach out in kindness.

Third, I would encourage you to stand up for fairness if you see another's rights being impeded. Elder L. Tom Perry was a great example of someone who firmly believed in man-woman marriage, and yet he was willing to stand up for the rights of others. He left an example of ensuring that others' rights were protected when he witnessed unfair treatment or an imbalance in our laws.

From the time of Joseph Smith to our present day, our legacy is one of reaching out to heal breaches and hurt without compromising the doctrine that is not ours to trade away.

There is a need for active involvement from your generation on this topic. I stand with the leaders of our Lord's Church when I say that we need your generation's natural understanding of compassion, respect, and fairness. We need your optimism and your determination to work through these complex social issues.

We have faith that you will turn to the Savior to understand how to live a Christlike life while also showing fairness and love to others who do not share your beliefs. We know you want to be a part of something meaningful, and we know that you are resilient and collaborative.

Most important, we need you to engage in dialogue regarding the complexities of this issue and find solutions for how to best extend fairness to everyone, including people of faith. These conversations need to be occurring in our schools, in our homes, and in our relationships with friends and coworkers.

When you have these conversations, please remember the principles we have discussed, which are simply these: see others through a lens of fairness, treat them with respect and kindness, and expect the same treatment in return.

APPLYING

THE

ATONEMENT

I surely don't understand all the meaning of the scriptural words "the pure love of Christ." But one meaning I do know is this: It is a gift we are promised when the Atonement of Jesus Christ has worked in us.

The gift is to want

what He wants.

When our love is the love He feels,
it is pure because He is pure.

—President Henry B. Eyring

THE ATONEMENT AND AGENCY
Elder D. Todd Christofferson

We must always remember that agency would have no meaning without the vital contribution of Jesus Christ. His central role began with His support of the Father's plan and His willingness to become the essential Savior under that plan. The plan required a setting for its implementation, and Jesus was instrumental in the creation of this planet for that purpose. Most important, while the Fall of Adam was a critical element of the plan, the Fall would also have frustrated the plan if certain of its consequences were not mitigated by the Atonement and Resurrection of Jesus Christ.

It was necessary in God's plan for our future happiness and glory that we become morally free and responsible. For that to happen, we needed an experience apart from Him where our own choices would determine our destiny. The Fall of Adam provided the spiritual death needed to separate us from God and place us in this mortal condition as well as the physical death needed to provide an end to the mortal experience. As Alma put it: "And now, ye see by this that our first parents were cut off both temporally and spiritually from the presence of the

Lord; and thus we see they became subjects to follow after their own will" (Alma 42:7).

Without more, however, these deaths would have defeated the plan after having made it possible. Death had to be permitted, but it also had to be overcome or we could not return to the presence of God. If our separation from God and our physical death were permanent, moral agency would mean nothing. Yes, we would be free to make choices, but what would be the point? The end result would always be the same no matter what our actions: death with no hope of resurrection and no hope of heaven. Good or bad as we might choose to be, we would all end up, in Jacob's words, "devils, angels to a devil" (2 Nephi 9:9).

With resurrection through Jesus Christ, the Fall can achieve its essential purpose without becoming a permanent death sentence. But there was one more thing that Christ needed to accomplish so that moral agency could have a positive potential. Just as death would doom us and render our agency meaningless but for the redemption of Christ, even so, without His grace, our bad choices or sins would leave us forever lost. There would be no way of fully recovering from our mistakes, and, being unclean, we could never live again in the presence of the "Man of Holiness" (Moses 6:57).

We cannot look to the law to save us when we have broken the law. We need a Savior, a Mediator who can overcome the effects of our sins and errors so that they are not necessarily fatal. It is because of the Atonement of Christ that we can recover from bad choices and be justified under the law as if we had not sinned.

THE ENABLING POWER OF THE ATONEMENT
Elder David A. Bednar

I suspect that you and I are much more familiar with the nature of the redeeming power of the Atonement than we are with the enabling power of the Atonement. It is one thing to know that Jesus Christ came to earth to *die* for us. That is fundamental and foundational to the doctrine of Christ. But we also need to appreciate that the Lord desires, through His Atonement and by the power of the Holy Ghost, to *live* in us—not only to direct us but also to empower us.

I think most of us know that when we do things wrong, when we need help to overcome the effects of sin in our lives, the Savior has paid the price and made it possible for us to be made clean through His redeeming power. Most of us clearly understand that the Atonement is for sinners. I am not so sure, however, that we know and understand that the Atonement is also for saints—for good men and women who are obedient and worthy and conscientious and who are striving to become better and serve more faithfully. I frankly do not think many of us "get it" concerning this enabling and strengthening aspect of the Atonement, and I wonder if we mistakenly believe we must make the journey from good to better and become a saint all by ourselves through sheer grit, willpower, and discipline, and with our obviously limited capacities.

The gospel of the Savior is not simply about avoiding bad in our lives; it also is essentially about doing and becoming good. And the Atonement provides help for us to overcome and avoid bad and to do and become good. There is help from the Savior for the entire journey of life—from bad to good to better and to change our very nature.

I am not trying to suggest that the redeeming and enabling powers of the Atonement are separate and discrete. Rather, these two dimensions of the Atonement are connected and complementary; they both need to be operational during all phases of the journey of life. And it is eternally important for all of us to recognize that *both* of these essential elements of the journey of life—both putting off the natural man and becoming a saint, both overcoming bad and becoming good—are accomplished through the power of the Atonement. Individual willpower, personal determination and motivation, and effective planning and goal setting are necessary but ultimately insufficient to triumphantly complete this mortal journey. Truly we must come to rely upon "the merits, and mercy, and grace of the Holy Messiah" (2 Nephi 2:8).

THE GOOD NEWS OF THE ATONEMENT
President Russell M. Nelson

Jesus was born to be Savior and Redeemer of all mankind (see Isaiah 49:26; 1 Nephi 10:5). He was the Lamb of God (see 1 Nephi 10:10), who offered Himself without spot or blemish (see 1 Peter 1:19) as a sacrifice for the sins of the world (see John 1:29). Later, as the resurrected Lord, He related that sacred responsibility to the meaning of *the gospel*, which He described in one powerful passage: "Behold I have given unto you my gospel, and this is the gospel which I have given unto you–that I came into the world to do the will of my Father, because my Father sent me. And my Father sent me that I might be lifted up upon the cross" (3 Nephi 27:13-14).

Thus Jesus personally defined *the gospel.* This term comes from the Old English *godspell,* which literally means "good news." "The good news is that Jesus Christ has made a perfect atonement for mankind that will redeem all mankind from the grave and reward each individual according to his/her works. This atonement was begun by his appointment in the premortal world but was worked out by Jesus during his mortal sojourn" (Bible Dictionary, s.v. "Gospels," 682).

Jesus fulfilled His glorious promise made in pre-earthly councils by atoning for the Fall of Adam and Eve unconditionally and for our sins upon the condition of our repentance. His responsibility as Savior and Redeemer was indelibly intertwined with His responsibility as Creator. To shed additional insight on this relationship, I would like to share a remarkable quotation that I found in a rare book in London one day while searching through the library of the British Museum. It was published as a twentieth-century English translation of an ancient Coptic text. It was written by Timothy, Patriarch of Alexandria, who died in A.D. 385. This record refers to the creation of Adam. Premortal Jesus is speaking of His Father:

"He . . . made Adam according to Our image and likeness, and He left him lying for forty days and forty nights without putting breath into him. And He heaved sighs over him daily, saying, 'If I put breath into this [man], he must suffer many pains.' And I said unto My Father, 'Put breath into him; I will be an advocate for him.' And My Father said unto Me, 'If I put breath into him, My beloved Son, Thou wilt be obliged to go down into the world, and to suffer many pains for him before Thou shalt have redeemed him, and made him to come back to his primal state.' And I said unto My Father, 'Put breath into him; I will be his advocate, and I will go down into the world, and will fulfil Thy command'" ("Discourse on Abbaton by Timothy, Archbishop of Alexandria," *Coptic Martyrdoms Etc. in the Dialect of Upper Egypt,* vol. 4 of *Coptic Texts*, edited, with English translations, by E. A. Wallis Budge [1914], 482; brackets appear in printed text).

Jesus's responsibility as Advocate, Savior, and Redeemer was foredetermined in premortal realms and fulfilled by His Atonement (see Job 19:25-26; Matthew 1:21). Your responsibility is to remember, to repent, and to be righteous.

THE SAVIOR'S PEACE
Elder D. Todd Christofferson

Years ago I presided in a Church disciplinary council. The man whose sins were the subject of the council sat before us and related something of his history. His sins were indeed serious, but he had also been terribly sinned against. As we considered

When we make mistakes—as we transgress and sin—we are able to overcome such weakness through the redeeming and cleansing power of the Atonement of Jesus Christ.

—ELDER DAVID A. BEDNAR

the matter, my soul was troubled, and I asked to be excused to think and pray about it alone before rejoining the council.

I was standing in front of a chair in my office pleading with the Lord to help me understand how such evil could have been perpetrated. I did not see but rather sensed an immense pit with a covering over it. One corner of the covering was lifted slightly for just an instant, and I perceived within it the depth and vastness of the evil that exists in this world. It was greater than I could really comprehend.

I was overcome. I collapsed into the chair behind me. It seemed to take my breath away. I cried silently, "How can we ever hope to overcome such evil? How can we survive something so dark and overwhelming?"

In that moment there came to my mind this phrase: "Be of good cheer; I have overcome the world" (John 16:33). Seldom have I felt such peace juxtaposed to the reality of evil. I felt a deeper appreciation for the intensity of the Savior's suffering, having a better, even frightening appreciation for the depth of what He had to overcome. I felt peace for the man who was before us for judgment, knowing he had a Redeemer whose grace was sufficient to cleanse him and also repair the injustices he had suffered. I knew better that good will triumph because of

Jesus Christ, whereas without Him we would have no chance. I felt peace, and it was very sweet.

THE STRENGTH OF THE LORD
Elder David A. Bednar

Nephi is an example of one who knew and understood and relied upon the enabling power of the Savior's Atonement. In 1 Nephi 7 we recall that the sons of Lehi had returned to Jerusalem to enlist Ishmael and his household in their cause. Laman and others in the party traveling with Nephi from Jerusalem back to the wilderness rebelled, and Nephi exhorted his brethren to have faith in the Lord. It was at this point in their trip that Nephi's brothers bound him with cords and planned his destruction. Please note Nephi's prayer in verse 17: "O Lord, according to my faith which is in thee, wilt thou deliver me from the hands of my brethren; yea, even *give me strength that I may burst these bands* with which I am bound" (emphasis added).

Do you know what I likely would have prayed for if I had been tied up by my brothers? My prayer would have included a request for something bad to happen to my brothers and ended with the phrase "wilt thou deliver me from the hands of my brethren" or, in other words, "Please get me out of this mess, now!" It is especially interesting to me that Nephi did not pray, as I probably would have prayed, to have his circumstances changed. Rather, he prayed for the strength to change his circumstances. And may I suggest that he prayed in this manner precisely because he knew and understood and had experienced the enabling power of the Atonement of the Savior.

I personally do not believe the bands with which Nephi was bound just magically fell from his hands and wrists. Rather, I suspect that he was blessed with both persistence and personal strength beyond his natural capacity, that he then "in the strength of the Lord" (Mosiah 9:17) worked and twisted and tugged on the cords and ultimately and literally was enabled to break the bands.

The implication of this episode for each of us is quite straightforward. As you and I come to understand and employ the enabling power of the Atonement in our personal lives, we will pray and seek for strength to change our circumstances rather than praying for our circumstances to be changed. We will become agents who "act" rather than objects that are "acted upon" (2 Nephi 2:14).

The enabling power of the Atonement of Christ strengthens us to do things we could never do on our own. Sometimes I wonder if in our latter-day world of ease—in our world of microwave ovens and cell phones and air-conditioned cars and comfortable homes–I wonder if we ever learn to acknowledge our daily dependence upon the enabling power of the Atonement.

FINDING

HAPPINESS

CHAPTER 11

Happiness has little to do with material wealth.

Nor does permanent from entertainment

*happiness come
or fun and games.*

Instead of being diversions
from an otherwise productive
life, these pursuits have become
all-consuming to many people.

—Elder Quentin L. Cook

THE MANNER OF HAPPINESS
Elder Jeffrey R. Holland

I do not think God in His glory or the angels of heaven or the prophets on earth intend to make us happy all the time, every day in every way, given the testing and trial this earthly realm is intended to provide. But my reassurance to you is that in God's plan we can do very much to find the happiness we do desire. We can take certain steps, we can form certain habits, we can do certain things that God and history tell us lead to happiness.

In short, your best chance for being happy is to do the things that happy people do. Live the way happy people live. Walk the path that happy people walk. And your chances to find joy in unexpected moments, to find peace in unexpected places, to find the help of angels when you didn't even know they knew you existed, improves exponentially. Here are at least a couple of ideas about how one might live "after the manner of happiness" (2 Nephi 5:27).

Above all else, ultimate happiness, true peace, and anything even remotely close to scriptural joy are found first, foremost, and forever in living the gospel of Jesus Christ. Lots of other philosophies and systems of belief have been tried.

Indeed it seems safe to say that virtually *every* other philosophy and system has been tried down through the centuries of history. But when the Apostle Thomas asked the Lord the question young people often ask today, "How can we know the way?" (and at your age in life that really translates, "How can we know the way to be happy?") Jesus gave the answer that rings from eternity to all eternity, "I am the way, the truth, and the life: . . . And whatsoever ye shall ask in my name, that will I do. . . . If ye shall ask any thing in my name, I will do it" (John 14:5-6, 13-14).

What a promise! Live my way, live my truth, live my life—live in this manner that I am showing you and teaching you—and whatsoever you ask will be given, whatsoever you seek you will find, including happiness. Parts of the blessing may come soon, parts may come later, and parts may not come until heaven, but they will come—all of them. What encouragement that is after a blue Monday or a sad Tuesday or a tearful Wednesday! And it is a promise the realization of which *cannot come any other way* than by devotion to eternal truth!

Second, learn as quickly as you can that so much of your happiness is in your hands, not in events or circumstances or fortune or misfortune. That is part of what the battle for agency was over in the premortal councils of heaven. We have choice, we have volition, we have agency, and we can choose if not happiness per se then we can choose to live after the manner of it. Don't be passive. Swim upward. Think and speak and act positively. That is what happy people do; that is one aspect of living after the manner of happiness.

Here is another. I have spent a long time trying to think if I have ever known a happy person who was unkind or unpleasant to be with. And guess what? I couldn't think of one, not a single, solitary one. So learn this great truth early in life: You can never, worlds without end, build your happiness on someone else's unhappiness. Sometimes, maybe especially when we are young and insecure and trying to make our way up in the world, we think if we can tear someone else down a little, it will somehow miraculously lift us up. That is what bullying is. That is what catty remarks are. That is what arrogance and superficiality and exclusiveness are. Perhaps we think if we are negative enough, or cynical enough, or just plain mean enough, then expectations won't be too high; we can keep everyone down to a flaw-filled level and therefore our flaws won't be so glaring.

Happy people aren't negative or cynical or mean, so don't plan on that being part of the "manner of happiness." If my life has taught me anything, it is that kindness and pleasantness and faith-based optimism are characteristics of happy people.

One last suggestion when there are so many others we should consider; that original verse from Nephi said that in an effort to find happiness in their new land after their thirty years of trouble, "I, Nephi, did cause my people to be industrious, and to labor with their hands" (2 Nephi 5:17). By contrast, those from whom they fled became "an idle people, full of mischief and subtlety" (2 Nephi 5:24).

If you want to be happy in school, or on a mission, or in a marriage—work at it. Learn to work. Serve diligently. Don't be idle and mischievous. A homespun definition of Christlike character might be the integrity to do the right thing at the right time in the right way.

TESTIMONY AND HAPPINESS
President Dieter F. Uchtdorf

Your testimony, or firm belief and assurance in your heart, will be a solid foundation, an overarching motive in all you accomplish in your life. It will be your true and faithful companion during good and challenging times in your lifelong transition. It will be a constant source of confidence and motivation. Your testimony provides you with a reason for gladness. It will help you cultivate a spirit of optimism and happiness and will help you to rejoice in the beauties of nature. Your testimony will help you to choose the right at all times and in all circumstances. It will give you peace of mind, His peace. If God is with you, who can be against you? (See Romans 8:31.)

OBEDIENCE AND FREEDOM
Elder Dale G. Renlund

We are all subject to spiritual laws. No one is exempt. We need to obey these spiritual laws, which we refer to as God's commandments.

Imagine fighting life's crosscurrents and crosswinds without spiritual stability. There is a reason obedience is the first law of heaven. Obedience is our choice. The Savior made this clear. As stated in the Joseph Smith Translation of Luke 14:28, Jesus directed, "Wherefore, settle this in your hearts, that ye will do the things which I shall teach, and command you."

It is that simple. Settle it. Decide now to be exactly obedient. As we do so, our spiritual stability will be greatly enhanced. We will avoid squandering God-given resources and making unproductive and destructive detours in our lives.

In 1980 my wife, daughter, and I moved to Baltimore, Maryland. Soon after our arrival we were invited to a ward

Obedience to God's laws preserves our freedom, flexibility, and ability to achieve our potential. The commandments are not intended to restrict us. Rather, obedience leads to increased spiritual stability and long-term happiness.

—ELDER DALE G. RENLUND

party at the home of a member. We were told it was to be a crab feast. We were excited, but we really didn't know what to expect. Our experience with seafood consisted of trout, canned salmon, and pickled herring. As we came to the member's backyard, we saw that newspapers had been spread on picnic tables and steaming bushels filled with red creatures the size of my fist had been dumped out on them.

We were informed that these were Maryland blue crabs, which turn bright red when they are steamed.

Ruth asked, "How do you catch them?"

We were told that early that morning, two of the brethren had gone to a butcher shop and purchased a bucket of chicken necks. As you know, chicken necks look like chicken and smell like chicken when cooked, but if that is what you are given for dinner, you will go hungry. The chicken neck consists of bone, tendon, and skin.

The assigned men had gone out in a skiff on the shallow Chesapeake Bay. In water about eight feet deep, they began the process of catching a crab. They tied a chicken neck to a string, dropped it into the water, and allowed it to settle on the sandy ocean floor. Sensing a potential feast, a crab scurried along the bottom and grabbed the chicken neck with its big claw. The men then slowly and steadily began pulling on the string. The crab held on to the chicken neck, and just as it was about to breach the surface of the bay, the crab became agitated and let go. But by that time the men had placed a small net under the crab. They took it out of the water and flung it into the boat. And, voilà: ward dinner!

Ruth said, "So, that's it? There's no hook? There's no rod? There's no reel?"

"That's right," they replied.

She said, "The crab could let go at any time?"

"Right."

"But they don't?"

"No," was the reply.

Ruth summed up this newfound knowledge by saying, "Boy, are those crabs stupid!"

If you were writing a pamphlet called *For the Strength of Young Crabs,* it would be pretty short, wouldn't it? It would say, "Lay off the chicken necks! They are a trap. Don't be fooled."

There are many chicken necks in the world: things that look enticing, things that look like a veritable feast, and things that seem worth a minor detour. But if we take that detour, we will, like the prodigal in the parable, experience a fleeting paroxysm of enjoyment followed by degradation ranging from slight to abysmal and misery ranging from small to unutterable before coming to ourselves and recognizing the mistake. The mistake is that these detours are traps.

We can look at each commandment separately and decide whether to obey or not, rationalize disobedience or not, or we can simply settle it in our hearts that we will do the things that the Lord teaches and commands. Nothing will give us greater freedom to accomplish our life's mission.

WILLINGNESS OF HEART
Elder Robert D. Hales

As members of the Church, we are striving to make the right choices for the right reasons. Early in our marriage I suggested that we pay our tithing from out of our year-end bonus, which came after the first of the year. I was thinking about tithing like life insurance or fire insurance—something you pay to stay out of trouble. But my sweet wife and companion taught me: "No," she said, "we will pay tithing as we go, because we love the Lord and want to build His kingdom."

Where the kingdom is concerned, the willingness of our hearts is everything. We keep the commandments because we love Heavenly Father and His Son, Jesus Christ. As we express that love, it is very simple. He said, "If ye love me, keep my commandments" (John 14:15). As we do, we lay the foundation of a great work.

THE FOUNDATION OF CHRIST
Elder Dale G. Renlund

Not too long ago, in the central part of the Democratic Republic of the Congo, Ruth and I met with a large number of Latter-day Saints who live in impoverished circumstances. I asked the assembled congregation, "What are your challenges?"

There was no response. I asked again. Again, there was no response. I asked a third time.

Finally, an older man stood slowly and asked me in all sincerity, "Elder Renlund, how can we have any challenges? We have the gospel of Jesus Christ."

Initially I felt like grabbing him and telling him to look around. They had nothing—no electricity and no running water. But then I understood. It is not what they possess that gives them strength; it is what they know. Their commitment to what they know gives them extraordinary spiritual stability. They keep the commandments. They are determined to be lifelong learners of spiritual things. They help each other. And they have Christ as their foundation.

WHEN BLESSINGS ARE DELAYED

CHAPTER 12

Do not rely on planning every
event of your life—even
every important event.

*Stand ready to accept
and the agency of
that inevitably*

the Lord's planning others in matters affect you.

Plan, of course, but fix your planning on personal commitments that will carry you through no matter what happens.

—Elder Dallin H. Oaks

THE LAW OF THE HARVEST
President Henry B. Eyring

Common sense tells you there is a law of the harvest, and so did the Savior and so have the prophets. Remember how Paul said it: "Be not deceived; God is not mocked: for whatsoever a man soweth, that shall he also reap. For he that soweth to his flesh shall of the flesh reap corruption; but he that soweth to the Spirit shall of the Spirit reap life everlasting" (Galatians 6:7-8).

But crops, even spiritual ones, are not all of one kind. There are early maturing varieties and late varieties. Maybe you've noticed in seed catalogues that one corn can be harvested in less, sometimes nearly half, the time it takes for another to be ready. You may not pay attention to that, but I do because I've lived in Rexburg, Idaho. It freezes there just before the Fourth of July, and sometimes just after.

Efforts, spiritual or practical, don't all bear fruit in the same length of time. You know that, but you may not have noticed something about your behavior that makes sense only if most of our experience is with early crops. Those are the ones where effort produces fast results. What happens after the early harvest? Would you expect an intelligent person to keep cultivating a field that had already produced its crop and been cleared? No, at least not in the hope of getting more harvest.

Now, one trouble with most of our struggles is that you can't see the seeds and the crops clearly. And you may not know as much about maturation time. All of us make decisions every day, almost every hour, about whether it's worth it to wait. The hardest ones are where the waiting includes working. Does it make sense to keep working, to keep sacrificing, when nothing seems to be coming from the effort?

There's a young man in the mission field who's made that choice in the last month. I heard his story, but there must have been thousands of such choices made last month. His companion would have made Job's critical friends seem like the Three Nephites. Just living and working with his companion required more contribution than the young missionary had dreamed he was going to have to make. The mission president authorized them to stay in their apartment because wind brought the effective temperature to 80 degrees below zero. So, the young man had to decide, "Shall we go out? We've been tracting and it's produced nothing. For what it would cost us, what would we get? We haven't got a contact, so we'd be just hitting doors." Well, he went–that's an odd investment decision, but he went. What he got was to meet one man, behind one of a hundred doors. In his letter about the man's baptism, he said, "I've never been more happy in my life."

ACCEPTING HIS WILL
Elder David A. Bednar

Righteousness and faith certainly are instrumental in moving mountains—if moving mountains accomplishes God's purposes and is in accordance with His will. Righteousness and faith certainly are instrumental in healing the sick, deaf, or lame—if such healing accomplishes God's purposes and is in accordance with His will. Thus, even with strong faith, many mountains will not be moved. And not all of the sick and infirm will be healed. If all opposition were curtailed, if all maladies were removed, then the primary purposes of the Father's plan would be frustrated.

Many of the lessons we are to learn in mortality can only be received through the things we experience and sometimes suffer. And God expects and trusts us to face temporary mortal adversity with His help so we can learn what we need to learn and ultimately become what we are to become in eternity.

A story to illustrate: John is a worthy priesthood holder and served faithfully as a full-time missionary. After returning home from his mission, he dated and married a righteous and wonderful young woman, Heather. John was twenty-three years old and Heather was twenty on the day they were sealed together for time and for all eternity in the house of the Lord. Please keep in mind the respective ages of John and Heather as this story unfolds.

Approximately three weeks after their temple marriage, John was diagnosed with bone cancer. As cancer nodules also were discovered in his lungs, the prognosis was not good.

John underwent a surgical procedure to remove a large tumor in his leg. He stated: "The surgery was a huge deal for us because pathology tests were to be run on the tumor to see how much of it was viable and how much of the cancer was dead. This analysis would give us the first indication of the effectiveness of the chemotherapy and of how aggressive we would need to be with future treatments."

Two days following the operation, I visited John and Heather in the hospital. We talked about the first time I met John in the mission field, about their marriage, about the cancer, and about the eternally important lessons we learn through the trials of mortality. As we concluded our time together, John asked if I would give him a priesthood blessing. I responded that I gladly would give such a blessing, but I first needed to ask some questions.

I then posed questions I had not planned to ask and had never previously considered: "[John,] do you have the faith not to be healed? If it is the will of our Heavenly Father that you are transferred by death in your youth to the spirit world to continue your ministry, do you have the faith to submit to His will and not be healed?"

I frankly was surprised by the questions I felt prompted to ask this particular couple. Frequently in the scriptures, the Savior or His servants exercised the spiritual gift of healing (see 1 Corinthians 12:9; D&C 35:9; 46:20) and perceived that an individual had the faith to be healed (see Acts 14:9; 3 Nephi 17:8; D&C 46:19). But as John and Heather and I counseled together and wrestled with these questions, we increasingly understood that if God's will were for this good young man to be healed, then that blessing could only be received if this valiant couple first had the faith not to be healed. In other words, John and Heather needed to overcome, through the Atonement of the Lord Jesus Christ, the "natural man" (Mosiah 3:19) tendency in all of us to demand impatiently and insist incessantly on the blessings we want and believe we deserve.

We recognized a principle that applies to every devoted disciple: strong faith in the Savior is submissively accepting of His will and timing in our lives–even if the outcome is not what we hoped for or wanted.

The Lord has His own timetable. "My words are sure and shall not fail," the Lord taught the early elders of this dispensation. "But," He continued, "all things must come to pass in their time" (D&C 64:31-32). The first principle of the gospel is faith in the Lord Jesus Christ. Faith means trust—trust in God's will, trust in His way of doing things, and trust in His timetable. We should not try to impose our timetable on His. Indeed, we cannot have true faith in the Lord without also having complete trust in the Lord's will and in the Lord's timing.

Someone has said that life is what happens to us while we are making other plans. Because of things over which we have no control, we cannot plan and bring to pass everything we desire in our lives. Many important things will occur in our lives that we have not planned, and not all of them will be welcome. Even our most righteous desires may elude us, or come in different ways or at different times than we have sought to plan.

For example, we cannot be sure that we will marry as soon as we desire. A marriage that is timely in our view may be our blessing or it may not. My wife Kristen is an example. She did not marry until many years after her mission and her graduation. Older singles have some interesting experiences. While she was at her sister's place to celebrate her fiftieth birthday, her sister's husband shared something he had just read in a newspaper. "Kristen," he said, "now that you are a single woman over fifty, your chances of marrying are not as good as your chances of being killed by a terrorist."

The timing of marriage is perhaps the best example of an extremely important event in our lives that is almost impossible to plan. Like other important mortal events that depend on the agency of others or the will and timing of the Lord, marriage cannot be anticipated or planned with certainty. We can and should work for and pray for our righteous desires, but, despite this, many will remain single well beyond their desired time for marriage.

So what should be done in the meantime? Faith in the Lord Jesus Christ prepares us for whatever life brings. This kind of faith prepares us to deal with life's opportunities—to take advantage of those that are received and to persist through the disappointments of those that are lost. In the exercise of that faith we should commit ourselves to the priorities and standards we will follow on matters we do not control and persist faithfully in those commitments whatever happens to us

Delayed blessings will build your faith in God to work, and wait, for Him.

—PRESIDENT HENRY B. EYRING

because of the agency of others or the timing of the Lord. When we do this, we will have a constancy in our lives that will give us direction and peace. Whatever the circumstances beyond our control, our commitments and standards can be constant.

LEARNING TO WAIT
President Henry B. Eyring

You are believers, not scoffers. Yet the scoffers can be helpful, because they encourage you to get an answer to this question: "What am I willing to keep giving heart and soul for, when neither I nor the scoffers may see returns for a long, long time?" And when we decide there are potential rewards worth that commitment, you'll want answers to another question: "How can I keep myself working and waiting if the scoffers are loud and the delay long?"

My guess is that all of us want to be better at working and waiting. Let me give you some advice about how to do it. It's not just theory; I got these hints from watching people who are the best I've seen at working and waiting. As the ads say, "This product has been proven in clinical tests."

All these hints have to do with where you focus your eyes. Two are things you ought to notice about the present, while you're working and waiting and not getting much yet in return.

And the last two are ways to look at the glorious future you're working and waiting for.

First, keep your eyes open for humor in the present. The people I know who are good for the long haul all seem to smile easily. You can't just get yourself a cheerful disposition, but you could keep your eyes open for something to smile at.

It's not hard. That's because the best humor springs from seeing the incongruity in your own predicament. Who's got more predicament than someone giving lots with small result? And who's more apt to laugh easily at himself than someone who has ultimate faith that the predicament will end? So look for the chance to smile.

The second place to focus your eyes is on the blessings you are getting now, while you wait. When you are trying hard to give, knowing the rewards will be delayed, it's terribly easy to overlook other blessings. Not all blessings are delayed. The early harvest is all around you. King Benjamin suggested you start by noticing that you are breathing. He also said, as you likely remember: "And secondly, he doth require that ye should do as he hath commanded you; for which if ye do, he doth immediately bless you; and therefore he hath paid you" (Mosiah 2:24).

Some results may be delayed to allow you to strengthen your faith. But other blessings come immediately. And King Benjamin valued those so highly compared to what we give that he said, in essence, "Mark your whole bill 'Paid in full.'" I know that it's hard to do if you are struggling under a heavy load. It's easy to see your load and to pine for the delayed rewards. But King Benjamin taught us that we're already abundantly paid, both with free gifts—such as life, for which we gave nothing—and with other blessings which have followed immediately upon our faithful service.

Among the reasons we ought to be thankful is that it will improve our vision. And with an eye on today's blessings you'll have more staying power for the distant goal.

Third, let me suggest how to keep your eye on the distant goal. What will a successful mission look like? How can I picture a great marriage? That's hard to see before you get there. And it's hard to persevere without some picture.

I've never forgotten the sacrament talk of an Englishman who had spent four years in a Japanese prison camp. Two missionaries had found and baptized him just before the capture of Singapore. He lost all his possessions save a photograph of the two missionaries. And that he kept hidden from his captors.

He survived, he said, largely by finding moments, sometimes hidden under a blanket, when he could look at the picture and imagine himself talking to the elders again.

You rarely can have a photograph of that future for which you now sacrifice, but you can get pictures. I suppose those pictures are really visions. And you'd have to pray for them, or take them as gifts. But at least watch for them. You may catch glimmers. I have had a few. And they help.

Fourth and finally, it's important to look carefully at those delayed blessings to notice that they are of at least two kinds. Some you can see and touch, and maybe even spend. For example, for keeping the Sabbath day, long enough, the promise is: "Verily I say, that inasmuch as ye do this, the fulness of the earth is yours, the beasts of the field and the fowls of the air, and that which climbeth upon the trees and walketh upon the earth" (D&C 59:16).

There are many promises of tangible things. And you and I know of instances where faithful performance seems not to have yet produced the blessings. But for all sacred performances in serving God, there is another promised blessing. You couldn't touch it or spend it, and you can only see it with special vision. But I commend developing the skill to see it.

A man named Helaman had such skill. He was struggling under great uncertainty about what was ahead. He was working and waiting. Here's what he said happened: "Yea, and it came to pass that the Lord our God did visit us with assurances that he would deliver us; yea, insomuch that he did speak peace to our souls, and did grant unto us great faith, and did cause us that we should hope for our deliverance in him" (Alma 58:11).

If you learn how to see it, you can know that many people have had that peace spoken to their souls. There are men and women undergoing trials and tests of faith that might lead you to say, "Their faith will break." But it doesn't break, and they do take it. And if you will look carefully, you will soon realize that peace has been spoken to their souls and faith in deliverance increased. If you notice that, it will make it more likely that you will feel that peace. I bear you my testimony that you can.

WHAT I DON'T KNOW—AND WHAT I DO
Elder David A. Bednar

I do not know why some people learn the lessons of eternity through trial and suffering—while others learn similar lessons through rescue and healing. I do not know all of the reasons, all of the purposes, and I do not know everything about the Lord's timing. With Nephi, you and I can say that we "do not know the meaning of all things" (1 Nephi 11:17).

But some things I absolutely do know. I know we are spirit sons and daughters of a loving Heavenly Father. I know the Eternal Father is the author of the plan of happiness. I know Jesus Christ is our Savior and Redeemer. I know Jesus enabled the Father's plan through His infinite and eternal Atonement. I know that the Lord, who was "bruised, broken, [and] torn for us" ("Jesus of Nazareth, Savior and King," *Hymns* [1985], no. 181), can succor and strengthen "his people according to their infirmities" (Alma 7:12). And I know one of the greatest blessings of mortality is to not shrink and to allow our individual will to be "swallowed up in the will of the Father" (Mosiah 15:7).

Though I do not know everything about how and when and where and why these blessings occur, I do know and I witness they are real. I testify that all of these things are true—and that we know enough by the power of the Holy Ghost to bear sure witness of their divinity, reality, and efficacy. My beloved brothers and sisters, I invoke upon you this blessing: even that as you press forward in your lives with steadfast faith in Christ, you will have the capacity to not shrink.

SPIRITUAL

GIFTS

CHAPTER 13

Being thankful is a spiritual gift.
It grows within us like faith
and charity.

*Being grateful for
God is portable,
through*

the goodness of and will go with us the veil.

It is a divine principle that will stay with us throughout eternity.

—Elder Neil L. Andersen

God is offended when we seek the gifts of the Spirit for our own purposes rather than for His. Our selfish motives may not be obvious to us. But few of us would be so blind as the man who sought to purchase the right to the gifts of the Spirit. You remember the sad story of a man named Simon and of Peter's rebuke:

"And when Simon saw that through laying on of the apostles' hands the Holy Ghost was given, he offered them money,

"Saying, Give me also this power, that on whomsoever I lay hands, he may receive the Holy Ghost.

"But Peter said unto him, Thy money perish with thee, because thou hast thought that the gift of God may be purchased with money.

"Thou hast neither part nor lot in this matter: for thy heart is not right in the sight of God.

"Repent therefore of this thy wickedness, and pray God, if perhaps the thought of thine heart may be forgiven thee.

"For I perceive that thou art in the gall of bitterness, and in the bond of iniquity.

"Then answered Simon, and said, Pray ye to the Lord for me, that none of these things which ye have spoken come upon me" (Acts 8:18-24).

Apparently Simon recognized his own corrupt motives. It may not be so easy for each of us. We almost always have more than one motive at a time. And some may be mixtures of what God wants as well as what we want. It is not easy to pull them apart.

For instance, consider yourself on the eve of a school examination or an interview for a new job. You know that the direction of the Holy Ghost could be of great help. I know from my own experience, for example, that the Holy Ghost knows some of the mathematical equations used to solve problems in thermodynamics, a branch of the sciences. I was a struggling physics student studying in a book that I still own. I keep it for historical and spiritual reasons. Halfway down a page (I could even show you where it is on the page), in the middle of some mathematics, I had a clear confirmation that what I was reading was true. It was exactly the feeling I had had come to me before as I pondered the Lord's scriptures and that I have had many times since. So I knew that the Holy Ghost understood whatever was true in what I might be asked on an examination in thermodynamics.

You can imagine that I was tempted to ask God to send me the Holy Ghost during the examination so I wouldn't need to study further. I knew that He could do it, but I did not ask Him. I felt that He would rather have me learn to pay a price in effort. He may well have sent help in the examination, but I was afraid that my motive might not be His. You have had that same choice to make often. It may have been when you were to be interviewed for a job. It may even have been when you were preparing for a talk or to teach a missionary discussion. Always there is the possibility that you may have a selfish purpose for yourself that is less important to the Lord.

For instance, I may want a good grade in a course, when He prefers that I learn how to work hard in the service of others. I may want a job because of the salary or the prestige, when He wants me to work somewhere else to bless the life of someone I don't even know yet. I have tried to suppress my desire and surrender to His.

When we feel our desire for people is moving toward being in line with His, that is one of the ways that we can know that we are being purified. When we pray for the gifts of the Spirit—and we should—one for which I pray is that I might have pure motives, to want what He wants for our Father's children and for me and to feel, as well as to say, that what I want is His will to be done.

Christlike attributes are natural consequences of developing and possessing *agape*, the pure love of Christ. If we can have and possess that one attribute, we do not need to try to achieve each of the other attributes enumerated separately by the Apostle Paul. Rather than focus on developing the fruits of this charity, our focus could be to develop charity itself.

The pure love of Christ or charity is selfless and self-sacrificing; it emanates from a pure heart and a good conscience. Charity is more than an act or action. Charity is an attitude, a state of heart and mind that accompanies one's actions. It is to be an integral part of one's nature. In fact, all things are to be done in charity. Charity casts out all fears and it is a prerequisite for entering the kingdom of heaven.

Conversion to Heavenly Father and Jesus Christ and His Atonement is the key to developing charity, the pure love of Christ. The development of charity then leads to the development of other Christlike attributes.

The First Presidency and the Quorum of the Twelve have stressed that the way to increase faith in Heavenly Father and Jesus Christ and His Atonement is to improve our Sabbath day observance at home and at church. Improved Sabbath day observance is vital to increasing our own conversion.

I promise you that as you make the Sabbath day a priority in your own life, your ability to feel *agape*, charity, this pure love of Christ, will increase. As you take time each week to prepare conscientiously for and worthily partake of the sacrament, you will see and feel the fruits of charity developing in yourself, in your very character, in your very being.

THE GIFT OF THE HOLY GHOST
Elder M. Russell Ballard

If you want to avoid the snares of Satan, if you need direction when the choices in front of you are puzzling and perplexing, learn to hear the voice of the Lord as communicated through the Holy Ghost. And then, of course, do what it tells you to do.

Nephi taught clearly that the Holy Ghost "is the gift of God unto all those who diligently seek him" and that "he that diligently seeketh shall find" (1 Nephi 10:17, 19). The stunning reality, my dear young brothers and sisters, is that you control how close you are to the Lord. You determine just how clear and readily available promptings from the Holy Ghost will be. You determine this by your actions, by your attitude, by the choices you make,

Plead with the Lord for the gift of discernment. Then live and work to be worthy to receive that gift so that when confusing events arise in the world, you will know exactly what is true and what is not.

—PRESIDENT RUSSELL M. NELSON

by the things you watch and wear and listen to and read, and by how consistently and sincerely you invite the Spirit into your life.

Contemplate for a moment the extent and the impact of this blessing! You have been given a gift that when exercised and respected will give you the answers to all of the confusing, thorny questions and problems you will face in your lives.

FAITH
Elder Neil L. Andersen

As evil increases in the world, there is a compensatory power, an additional spiritual endowment, a revelatory gift for the righteous.

This added blessing of spiritual power does not settle upon us just because we are part of this generation. It is willingly offered to us; it is eagerly put before us. But as with all spiritual gifts, it requires our desiring it, pursuing it, and living worthy of receiving it. "For what doth it profit a man if a gift is bestowed upon him, and he receive not the gift?" (D&C 88:33).

Faith is the muscle of spiritual knowledge and power. Faith is a spiritual gift of God, but it is developed and magnified as we eagerly pursue our journey of embracing and following the Savior. I remember once long ago, before I was serving as a General Authority, having a man approach me whom I had known for some time in business. We talked about a challenge he was facing in his life, and I gave him some of my thoughts.

He then said to me, "Neil, you have something I don't have. You have faith in God."

The way he said it to me, I sensed he felt that having faith was not something chosen or determined by me or by him but that somewhere in the lottery of life my gene pool had brought a quality of believing and trusting in God that his gene pool had not. This, my brothers and sisters, is not a correct notion of faith in God or faith in Christ.

Our Heavenly Father desires that faith will grow within the hearts of all His sons and daughters. As one repents, opens her heart, or seeks to strengthen his faith, the Lord is magnanimous and generous in return. Alma said, "Remember, that God is merciful unto all who believe on his name" (Alma 32:22). You of course will remember that Alma talked about arousing our faculties, experimenting upon the words of Christ, and exercising faith to give additional place for faith to grow (see Alma 32).

Never forget that the seed must be nourished. We need to help those we love to understand that faith is not stagnant. It is either growing or it is diminishing. We have all been taught these things. Faith grows by repentance and obedience, by prayer and scripture study, by attending church and taking the sacrament, and by serving and associating with other believers.

SEEKING AFTER SPIRITUAL GIFTS
Elder David A. Bednar

Faith is not a trait to be developed nor a reward to be earned. Rather, it is a gift we receive from God. Scriptural synonyms for faith include trust, confidence, and reliance. Thus, the spiritual gift of faith enables us to trust in Christ and to have confidence in His power to cleanse, renew, and redeem us. Faith means we are beginning to rely upon His merits, mercy, and grace (see 2 Nephi 2:8; 31:19; Moroni 6:4). Indeed you and I have a responsibility to appropriately seek after this gift, and we must do all that we can do to qualify for the gift of faith. Ultimately, however, the gift is bestowed upon us by a loving and caring God.

The Holy Ghost delivers the spiritual gift of faith. Obedience and righteousness invite the companionship of the third member of the Godhead. Sin and wickedness repulse the Holy Ghost and make it impossible for Him to deliver spiritual gifts. Can you begin to see why our covenant to obey the commandments is so important?

THE POWER OF HONESTY
Elder Neil L. Andersen

God our Father and His Son, Jesus Christ, are beings of absolute, perfect, and complete honesty and truth. Honesty describes the character of God, and therefore honesty is at the very heart of our spiritual growth and spiritual gifts (see Isaiah 65:16).

There is enormous spiritual power in remaining true and honest when the consequences of your honesty could appear to be a disadvantage. Each of you will face such decisions. These defining moments will test your integrity. As you choose honesty and truth–whether or not the situation works out the way you hope–you will realize that these important crossroads become fundamental pillars of strength in your spiritual growth.

As you humbly ponder and pray about your own desire to be honest and quietly make decisions that lift your personal integrity, I promise that you will have greater clarity come into your life. You will feel the grace of the Savior as He leads you along to ever greater honesty, assuring you of His love and approval. As you are honest, you will know that He is aware of you. He will bless you as you seek to be like Him.

BUILDING HEALTHY RELATIONSHIPS

Be the kind of person who stands loyally by the principles and people and institutions to which you have declared allegiance, and that probably have given you most of the blessings you enjoy.

How far is too far discouraged friend, or a troubled

to walk with a
or a struggling spouse,
child?

When the opposition heats up and
the going gets tough, how much of
what we thought was important to
us will we defend?

—Elder Jeffrey R. Holland

THE BLESSING OF GOOD FRIENDS
Elder Ronald A. Rasband

In my youth, an inspired patriarch laid his hands on my head and by revelation opened to me an understanding of my potential—for who I really am—and gave a direction for my life, just like a patriarch has done for most of you. I was told that I would not lack for friends and associates, that their friendship would be a special blessing to me both temporally as well as spiritually. I was counseled to select for my closest friends those who were righteous and had a desire to keep the commandments of God.

That passage from my patriarchal blessing and the verse from Doctrine and Covenants 121 that reminds Joseph Smith, "Thy friends do stand by thee" (v. 9), have been like a comfort blanket to me throughout my life. At times, especially while living away from home, those words have given me a peace and strength—my friends were standing by, although separated by many miles. And at such times I learned one of life's most important lessons, that no matter how long I was away, no matter how great the distance, whenever my friends and I met again, it was as if nothing had changed. We picked up our lives where we left off, and it was as if time had stood still.

Why do I emphasize that? Because in today's world so

many people willingly trade those friendships for video characters and quick text messages. They spend their time identifying with television personalities who for them are only faces on a screen. They are choosing to "hang out" rather than commit to a deep and meaningful relationship that can be sealed in the temple for eternity.

From my earliest days growing up in the Cottonwood Stake in the Salt Lake Valley, friends have been a special blessing to me. The closest friends made in my youth remain my friends to this day. It has always been that way; we have always been there for each other. And I have been grateful to make new friends who have been a strength and blessing to me as well.

THE INFLUENCE OF FRIENDS
President Thomas S. Monson

In a survey which was made in selected wards and stakes of the Church, we learned a most significant fact. Those persons whose friends married in the temple usually married in the temple, while those persons whose friends did not marry in the temple usually did not marry in the temple. The influence of one's friends appeared to be a more dominant factor than parental urging, classroom instruction, or proximity to a temple.

We tend to become like those whom we admire. Just as in

Nathaniel Hawthorne's classic account "The Great Stone Face," we adopt the mannerisms, the attitudes, even the conduct of those whom we admire—and they are usually our friends. Associate with those who, like you, are planning not for temporary convenience, shallow goals, or narrow ambition but rather for those things that matter most—even eternal objectives.

THE FRIENDS I DIDN'T REACH
Elder Jeffrey R. Holland

I wish I could go back to my youth and there have another chance to reach out to those who, at the time, didn't fall very solidly onto my radar scope. We are so vulnerable in our youth. We want to feel included and important, to have the feeling we matter to others. In your years people deserve to have true friendships—the real value of which, like our health, may never be realized until we face life without them. I think that my problem was not that I had too few friends but almost too many—maybe more friends than anyone I know. But it is the associations I didn't have, the friends I didn't reach that cause me some pain now all these years later.

I have wept for people in our youth for whom I and a lot of others obviously were *not* masters of "the healer's art" ("Lord, I Would Follow Thee," *Hymns* [1985], no. 220). We simply were not the Savior's agents or disciples that He intended a group of young people to be. I cannot help but wonder what I might have done to watch out a little more for the ones not included, to make sure the gesture of a friendly word or a listening ear or a little low-cost casual talk and shared time might have reached far enough to include those hanging on the outer edge of the social circle, and in some cases barely hanging on at all.

Jesus said in the culmination of His most remarkable sermon ever: "For if ye love them which love you, what reward have ye? do not even the publicans the same? And if ye salute your brethren only, what do ye more than others? do not even the publicans so?" (Matthew 5:46-47).

It is with some sorrow that I acknowledge I have never known what it is like not to have a date when everyone else had one, nor to be painfully shy, nor to be chosen last for basketball, nor to be truly poor, nor to face the memories and emotions of a broken home—nor any one of a hundred other things I know many have had to contend with in the past or are contending with right now. In acknowledging that, I make an appeal for us to reach beyond our own contentment, to move out of our own comfort and companion zone, to reach those who may not always be so easy to reach.

If we do less, what distinguishes us from the biblical publican? I might not have been able to heal all the wounds of those I met in my young adult years—your years—but I can't help think that if I had tried even harder to be more of a healer, more of a helper, a little less focused on myself, and a little more centered on others, some days in the lives of those God placed in my path would have been much better. "I have called you friends," the Savior said in one of His highest compliments to His disciples (John 15:15). Therefore, "love one another, as I have loved you" (v. 12). That harvest is great and the laborers are few.

PERSONAL INTERACTION
Elder M. Russell Ballard

Honestly, how much time do you spend every day on your cell phone or tablet, not including school or Church work?

Their use is appropriate, and they are a blessing. However, when smartphones begin to interfere with our relationships with friends and family—and even more importantly, with God—we need to make a change. For some of you, the adjustment will be slight; for others, it may be significant.

I am also concerned that excessive text messaging, Facebooking, tweeting, and Instagraming are replacing talking—talking directly one to another and talking in prayer

The friends you choose
will either help or hinder
your success.

—PRESIDENT THOMAS S. MONSON

with our Heavenly Father and thinking about the things that matter most in life.

Too often, young people find themselves in the same room with family or friends but are busy communicating with someone not present, thereby missing an opportunity to visit with those nearby. When this happens, maybe you need to leave the room and send a text message back to them to get their attention!

CHOOSING FRIENDS WISELY
Elder Robert D. Hales

Our friends are important at all times, especially in times of need when we are depressed with feelings of loneliness and despair. Choosing our friends wisely is important. In times of trouble, do your friends stand by you? What kind of a friend or companion are you?

Often we choose our friends by their physical appearance and personalities. The best dancer, the most fashionable, the same geographic home area (city or rural, east or west), the most athletic, the sharpest car, the most handsome, the most beautiful, the most charming personality, the most intelligent, the richest, or the poorest are just a few of the criteria for selecting dates or friends. These are all superficial.

The first test of friendship and companionship is knowing

that in their company it is easier to live according to the commandments you have been taught and know are important to happiness.

The second test of real friendship and companionship is whether you are asked as a condition of their friendship or companionship to choose between their way and the Lord's way. For example, true friendship does not exist if a condition of that friendship is to participate in breaking moral laws or the Word of Wisdom with phrases like: "Try it just once," "Everyone does it," "Who is going to know?" "Show me that you really love me."

Those who are alone and lonely should not retreat to the sanctuary of their private thoughts and chambers. Such retreat will ultimately lead them into the darkening influence of the adversary, which leads to despondency, loneliness, frustration, and to thinking of themselves as worthless. After one thinks of himself as worthless, he then ofttimes turns to associates who corrode delicate spiritual contacts, rendering the person's spiritual receiving antennas and transmitters useless. What good is it to associate with and ask advice of someone who is disoriented himself and only tells us what we want to hear? Isn't it better to turn to loving parents, friends, and associates who can help us reach for and attain celestial goals?

Consider the love your parents have for you and that you have for them. Instead of simply asking them, "Where are the keys to your car?" you might add, "I'll be a bit late tonight." Often the clock ticks more loudly and the hands move more slowly when the night is dark, the hour is late, and a son or a daughter has not yet come home. A telephone call—"We're okay; we just stopped for something to eat. Don't worry; we're fine"—is an indication of true love for parents.

Let me relate a tender yet simple experience. Each time I would visit Mattie, a dear friend and an older widow whom I had known for many years and whose bishop I had been, my heart grieved at her utter loneliness. One of her sons lived many miles away, halfway across the country, but he rarely visited her. He would come to Salt Lake, take care of business matters, see his brothers and sisters, and leave for his own home without visiting his mother. When I would call to see this mother, she would make an excuse for her boy and tell me just how busy he was.

The years passed. The loneliness deepened. Then one afternoon I received a telephone call. That special son was in Salt Lake

City. A change had occurred in his life. He had become imbued with a desire to help others, to adhere more faithfully to God's commandments. He was proud of his newfound ability to cast off the old man and become new and useful. He wanted to come immediately to my office that he might share with me the joy in service that he now felt. With all my heart I wanted to welcome him and to extend my personal congratulations. Then I thought of his grieving mother, that lonely widow, and suggested, "Dick, I can see you at four o'clock this afternoon, provided you visit your dear mother before coming here." He agreed.

Just before our appointment, a call came to me. It was that same mother. There was an excitement in her voice that words cannot adequately describe. She exuded enthusiasm even over the phone and declared proudly, "Bishop, you'll never guess who has just visited me." Before I could answer, she exclaimed, "Dick was here! My son Dick has spent the past hour with me. He is a new man. He has found himself. I'm the happiest mother in the world!" Then she paused and quietly spoke: "I just knew he would not really forget me."

Years later, at Mattie's funeral, Dick and I spoke tenderly of that experience. We had witnessed a glimpse of God's healing power through the window of a mother's faith in her son.

KEEP

TRYING

If you move forward with bold faith, you are most likely going to have a few failures in your life.

You are going a few scrapes

to take
and bruises.

There will be dark patches on the
road ahead. But you are sons and
daughters of God. As such, you have an
inexhaustible, divine source of strength
burning inside of you.

—Elder Gary E. Stevenson

I wish to bear witness of God's power of deliverance. At some point in our lives we will all need that power. Every person living is in the midst of a test. We have been granted by God the precious gift of life in a world created as a proving ground and a preparatory school. The tests we will face, their severity, their timing, and their duration will be unique for each of us. But two things will be the same for all of us. They are part of the design for mortal life.

First, the tests at times will stretch us enough for us to feel the need for help beyond our own. And, second, God in His kindness and wisdom has made the power of deliverance available to us.

Now you might well ask, "Since Heavenly Father loves us, why does His plan of happiness include trials that could overwhelm us?" It is because His purpose is to offer us eternal life. He wants to give us a happiness that is only possible as we live as families forever in glory with Him. And trials are necessary for us to be shaped and made fit to receive that happiness that comes as we qualify for the greatest of all the gifts of God.

Some of you may feel the pressures of those tests now, but

all of us will face them. It helps to know that they do not come from random chance or from a cruel God. And knowing what a wonderful reward lies ahead helps to endure the tests well.

OVERCOMING OBSTACLES
President Dieter F. Uchtdorf

After the turmoil of the Second World War, my family ended up in Russian-occupied East Germany. We had fled from Czechoslovakia before the Russian front and lost everything during this terrible war. In the town of Zwickau, East Germany, my family learned about the restored gospel and joined the Church. At that time I was only six years old and the youngest of four children. The Church made an indescribable difference in our then very difficult lives. Even in these trying times, with extreme financial hardship, we were a happy family because of the Church.

Later, as a ten-year-old boy, I attended fourth grade and had to learn Russian as my first foreign language. Initially it was quite difficult because of the Cyrillic alphabet, but as time went on I seemed to manage all right.

When I turned eleven, we had to leave East Germany overnight because of the political orientation of my father. He was perceived as a dissenter by the Communist government, and his life was endangered. We were refugees again and had lost everything for the second time.

Now I was going to school in West Germany, and the Russian language was not appreciated there at all. We were in the American-occupied part of Germany, and in school I had to learn English. Somehow I could not learn it. To learn Russian was difficult, but English was impossible. I even thought my mouth was not made for speaking English. My teachers had a hard time. My parents were desperate. And I knew English was not my language.

I agonized through those school years, helped and encouraged by kind and understanding English teachers, but I just couldn't do it. It wasn't my thing!

At this time, my dream in life was to become a pilot. Almost daily I rode my bicycle to the airport. I could picture myself in the cockpit of an airliner or even in a military jet fighter. This was definitely my thing!

I eventually learned that to become a pilot, I needed to speak English. Suddenly, the resisting condition of my mouth changed. I was able to learn the language. Why? Because of a strong motive!

WHEN ANSWERS DON'T COME QUICKLY
Elder David A. Bednar

Jesus Christ knows and loves us individually. He is concerned about our spiritual development and progress, and He encourages us to grow through the exercise of inspired, righteous, and wise judgment. The Redeemer will never leave us alone. We should always pray for guidance and direction. We should always seek for the constant companionship of the Holy Ghost. But we should not be dismayed or discouraged if answers to our petitions for direction or help do not necessarily come quickly. Such answers rarely come all at once. Our progress would be hindered and our judgment would be weak if every answer was given to us immediately and without requiring the price of faith, work, study, and persistence.

HUMILITY AND DELIVERANCE
President Henry B. Eyring

The Lord always wants to lead us to deliverance through our becoming more righteous. That requires repentance. And that takes humility. So the way to deliverance always requires humility in order for the Lord to be able to lead us by the hand where He wants to take us through our troubles and on to sanctification.

The humility you and I need to get the Lord to lead us by the hand comes from faith. It comes from faith that God really lives, that He loves us, and that what He wants—hard as it may be—will always be best for us.

The Savior showed us that humility. You have read of how He prayed in the garden while He was suffering a trial on our behalf beyond our ability to comprehend or to endure, or even for me to describe. You remember His prayer: "Father, if thou be willing, remove this cup from me: nevertheless not my will, but thine, be done" (Luke 22:42).

He knew and trusted His Heavenly Father, the great Elohim. He knew that His Father was all-powerful and infinitely kind. The Beloved Son asked for the power of deliverance to help Him in humble words like those of a little child.

The Father did not deliver the Son by removing the trial. For our sakes He did not do that, and He allowed the Savior to finish the mission He came to perform. Yet we can forever take courage and comfort from knowing of the help that the Father did provide: "And there appeared an angel unto him from heaven, strengthening him" (Luke 22:43).

The Savior prayed for deliverance. What He was given was not an escape from the trial but comfort enough to pass through it gloriously. From this you have counsel for passing the physical and spiritual tests of life. You will need God's help after you have done all you can for yourself.

TURNING TO GOD DAILY
Elder D. Todd Christofferson

Some time before I was called as a General Authority, I faced a personal economic challenge that persisted for several years. It did not come about as a consequence of anyone's wrongdoing or ill will. It was just one of those things that sometimes come into our lives.

It ebbed and flowed in seriousness and urgency, but it never went away completely. At times, this challenge threatened the welfare of my family and me.

I prayed for some miraculous intervention to deliver us. Although I offered that prayer many times with great sincerity and earnest desire, the answer in the end was no. Finally, I learned to pray as the Savior did, "Nevertheless not my will, but thine, be done" (Luke 22:42).

I sought the Lord's help with each tiny step along the way to a final resolution. There were times when I had exhausted all my resources, when I had nowhere or no one to turn to at that moment, when there was simply no other human being I could call on to help meet the exigency before me. With no other recourse, more than once, I fell down before my Heavenly Father begging in tears for His help. And He did help.

Sometimes it was nothing more than a sense of peace, a feeling of assurance that things would work out. I might not see how or what the path would be, but He gave me to know that, directly or indirectly, He would open the way. Circumstances might change. A new and helpful idea might come to mind. Some unanticipated income or other resource might appear at just the right time. Somehow there was a resolution.

Though I suffered then, as I look back now, I'm grateful that there was not a quick solution to my problem. The fact that I was forced to turn to God for help almost daily over an extended period of years taught me truly how to pray and get answers to prayer, and taught me in a very practical way to have faith in God. I came to know my Savior and my Heavenly Father in a way and to a degree that might not have happened otherwise, or that might have taken me much longer to achieve.

I learned that daily bread is a precious commodity. I learned that manna today can be as real as the physical manna of biblical history. I learned to trust in the Lord with all my heart. I learned to walk with Him, day by day.

Whenever we are inclined to feel burdened down with the blows of life, let us remember that others have passed the same way, have endured, and then have overcome. When we have done all that we are able, we can rely on God's promised help.

—PRESIDENT THOMAS S. MONSON

OPPOSITION FOLLOWING ENLIGHTENMENT
Elder Jeffrey R. Holland

I wish to encourage every one of you regarding opposition that so often comes *after* enlightened decisions have been made, *after* moments of revelation and conviction have given us a peace and an assurance we thought we would never lose. In his letter to the Hebrews, the Apostle Paul was trying to encourage new members who had just joined the Church, who undoubtedly had had spiritual experiences and had received the pure light of testimony, only to discover that not only had their troubles not ended, but that some of them had only begun.

The reminder is that we cannot sign on for a moment of such eternal significance and everlasting consequence without knowing it will be a fight–a good fight and a winning fight, but a fight nevertheless. Paul said to those who thought a new testimony, a personal conversion, or a spiritual baptismal experience would put them beyond trouble, "Call to remembrance the former days, in which, *after ye were illuminated,* ye endured a great fight of afflictions" (Hebrews 10:32; emphasis added).

Then came this tremendous counsel, which is at the heart of my counsel to you: "Cast not away therefore your confidence, *which hath great recompence of reward.* For ye have need of patience, that, after ye have done the will of God, ye might receive the promise. . . . If any man draw back, my soul shall have no pleasure in him. . . . We are not of them who draw back unto perdition" (Hebrews 10:35-36, 38-39; emphasis added).

In LDS talk that is to say, "Sure it is tough–before you join the Church, while you are trying to join, and after you have joined." That is the way it has always been, Paul said, but don't "draw back," he warned. Don't panic and retreat. Don't lose your confidence. Don't forget how you once felt. Don't distrust the experience you had.

I suppose every returned missionary and probably every convert within the sound of my voice knows exactly what I am talking about: appointments for discussions canceled, the Book of Mormon in a plastic bag hanging from a front-door knob, baptismal dates not met. And so it goes through the teaching period, through the commitments, through the baptism, through the first weeks and months in the Church, and more or less forever. At least the adversary would pursue it forever, if he thought he could see any weakening of your resolve or any chink in your armor–even if it is after the fact.

I acknowledge the reality of opposition and adversity, but I bear witness of the God of Glory, of the redeeming Son of God, of light and hope and a bright future. I promise you that God lives and loves you, each one of you, and that He has set bounds and limits to the opposing powers of darkness. I testify that Jesus is the Christ, the victor over death and hell and the fallen one who schemes there.

"Fear ye not." And when the second and the third and the fourth blows come, "fear ye not. . . . The Lord shall fight for you" (Exodus 14:13-14).

DON'T BE DISCOURAGED
Elder Neil L. Andersen

My wife, Kathy, and I were once traveling back from Guatemala City with a connecting flight in Miami, Florida. We had an important appointment, and it was vital that we catch the plane in Miami. We started early that morning, but as we traveled into Guatemala City, the traffic was unusually congested. We were concerned about reaching the airport on time. We arrived with just enough time to catch our plane.

We rushed through immigration and toward the departure gate. At the gate, we learned that our plane would not be leaving for an hour and a half. It had arrived late the night before in turbulent weather. The pilots and crew were required to have a certain amount of time to rest. With this delay, we worried about making our connection in Miami. We boarded the plane an hour and a half later, but, after backing away from the gate, we learned that there was an electronic malfunction in the cockpit. This delayed us another forty minutes. We took a deep breath, wondering if there was any possibility of making our connection.

The plane made good time between Guatemala City and Miami. We arrived in Miami with only thirty minutes before our connecting plane was scheduled to leave. We headed for U.S. Customs, silently praying that the luggage we were pulling behind us would not be chosen for inspection. Our prayers were answered. Glancing at the airport monitors, I noted that our airplane was at Gate D-3. After running to the D concourse came the painful process of security screening: Off with the shoes. Liquids in a plastic bag. Laptop separate. Hope that the security monitor doesn't buzz when moving through the screener.

Completing the security check, we had only ten minutes before the scheduled departure. I looked up at the monitor again. To my horror, I had made a mistake–the plane was not leaving from D-3 but from E-3. We were in the wrong concourse. We were out of breath. The plane doors were probably already closed, and we were several hundred yards away. We thought about giving up. But, receiving encouragement from each other, we pushed ourselves toward the finish. Off we sprinted, rolling bags right behind. As we rounded the turn to Gate E-3, we heard them call our names. It was a miracle. The door was still open. We made it!

Your spiritual destiny will have obstacles, delays, and equipment malfunctions. There will be mistakes. You may wonder if you are going to make it. Don't be discouraged! You will also have moments of hope and faith as doors open and obstacles are overcome. Continue, persist, above all, believe in Christ and learn to follow Him and His prophets; endure, as Nephi said, with a "brightness of hope" (2 Nephi 31:20). As you do, I promise you, one day you will hear your name. You will make it.

HANDLING HOPELESS SITUATIONS
President Dieter F. Uchtdorf

Sometimes it is difficult to see what good will come out of your efforts and where the road you are on will lead to. You might even feel like Paul on his way to Rome. In the book of Acts we read that Paul was taken as a prisoner to the capital city of the world's number-one military power. It looked bleak for the Apostle Paul. En route to Rome the ship he was on was caught in a *perfect storm,* one not made in Hollywood but in the Mediterranean Sea. All their lives were endangered. We read, "And when neither sun nor stars in many days appeared, and no small tempest lay on us, all hope that we should be saved was then taken away" (Acts 27:20).

How did Paul handle this hopeless situation? Amidst all this commotion, he stood up and said, "Be of good cheer: . . . For there stood by me this night the angel of God, whose I am, and whom I serve, Saying, Fear not" (Acts 27:22-24). Paul then gave concise instructions that appeared at the moment far removed from a logical problem-solving process. Among other things, he told them to lighten the ship, and they did so by throwing things they cherished overboard. Then "they committed themselves unto the sea . . . , and hoised up the mainsail to the wind, and made toward shore" (Acts 27:40). Fortunately the guards who were prepared to kill Paul believed his words and followed his counsel. The scripture reports, "And so it came to pass, that they escaped all safe to land" (Acts 27:44).

There will be times in your lives when you will not know the quick answers for your circumstances. Rely then on the word of God. Your Father in Heaven will always teach you to fear not, but to be of good cheer, to lighten your ship of clutter and focus on the spiritual matters, to commit yourselves to the covenants you made, and to put your sail of righteousness into the wind and head courageously toward the land of your eternal future.

The excerpts in this book come from messages delivered specifically to young adult audiences in a variety of settings, from devotionals to commencement addresses to firesides. A complete list of those sources can be found at LDSLiving.com/withyou.